DOVER'S
CAVES AND TUNNELS

Part of our rich heritage

by Derek Leach OBE

Dedicated to all the Royal Engineers
who tunnelled in the Dover area during the last two hundred years.

Copyright Derek Leach 2011

Published in 2011 by Riverdale Publications
24 Riverdale, River, Dover, CT17 0QX

ISBN 978-0-9536166-9-5

Printed in England by A. R. Adams (Printers) Ltd.
The Printing House, Dour Street, Dover CT16 1EW

Contents

Foreword iv

Introduction vi

PART ONE: MILITARY PURPOSES

Chapter 1 Dover Castle 1

Chapter 2 Western Heights 21

Chapter 3 Other underground military installations 33

PART TWO: CIVILIAN PURPOSES

Chapter 1 Descriptions of civilian caves and tunnels 57

Chapter 2 First World War Caves, Tunnels and Shelters 87

Chapter 3 Second World War Caves, Tunnels and Shelters 93

Chapter 4 Wartime Memories 109

Acknowledgements 117

Sources of information 118

Index of caves and tunnels 120

Foreword

Why produce a book about Dover's caves and tunnels? Like most people in Dover I knew of the tunnels under the castle and had visited those open to the public. I also knew of some of those in Snargate Street. But I had little idea of how many or where every cave and tunnel was located or what they looked like or how they had originated. I could have remained in fairly blissful ignorance until I looked at a file inherited from that great Dover researcher, Joe Harman, entitled caves and tunnels. For once, this file of Joe's was almost empty except for one plan of a Dover tunnel complex and a phone number for JW. I then remembered that Joe had once said to me that if I wanted to know anything about Dover's tunnels then John Walton was the man. Looking for another book subject, I contacted John and visited him when I was shown an amazing number of tunnel plans either drawn by him in the 1970s or acquired since from other sources. He had an amazing story to tell, which convinced me that a book was needed.

With so many caves and tunnels in the Dover area the fire service practised for tunnel fires, often using the underground works at St Martin's Battery. A dummy would be put in the tunnel, paper would then be set alight inside and firemen would have to rescue the dummy and put out the fire. A real underground fire in October 1969 was much more serious. Called to a fire in a former military underground site at St Margaret's, which lasted two days, firemen had to work in intense smoke and heat, using vast quantities of high expansion foam with no prior knowledge of the entrances, construction or extent of the workings and not knowing whether anybody was trapped inside.

Following this fire, two Dover firemen, John Walton and Allen Cook (known as Sam by all his mates), assisted by others from time to time, decided to survey and record all the known underground sites for the use of the Fire Brigade. Undertaken in their spare time over 18 months they located, visited, recorded and mapped. Much of the work was physical, exploring the interiors of tunnels and complexes, but much time was also spent beforehand tracing the owners, including private owners, local authorities and government departments. Finding and listening to people with local knowledge was also profitable.

Wherever possible a record was made of the location, landmarks, type of system, entry and exit points, age if known, ventilation points, the number and dimensions of, what in some cases, were a maze of tunnels, length, construction (ranging from bare chalk to steel, concrete or brick lined) and particular hazards. This information could be vital in the event of a fire, reducing the risk to firemen and assisting in the search for the source of the fire or people trapped.

Meticulous drawings of 24 sites were eventually made and handed to Kent Fire Brigade for operational use. The work of John and Sam did not stop there. They continued to survey other sites and to acquire existing drawings of many more.

Concerned about the many military underground sites, John and Sam contacted Shorncliffe army base for information and were invited to the drawing office. They arrived just in time because the contents of a shed containing Second World War drawings were about to be rubbished. Instead, they were given to the firemen.

Something similar happened when they visited Archcliffe Fort which was still an army depot at the time. There were drawings, but, unfortunately, some of them were marked 'Secret', but the guy said not to worry and promptly tore off the Secret stamp and gave the drawings to John and Sam!

John Walton would not allow me to use any of his plans fearful that anybody reading my book would be tempted to explore some of the tunnels for themselves and possibly injure themselves (although the plans have found their way on to the internet anyway). I have respected his wishes, but with his agreement have obtained the original set produced for the Fire Brigade from other sources. Many of the tunnel entrances are sealed, whilst others may be explored with the owners' permission.

Unlike the vandals who deface and destroy when they enter these tunnels, there are enthusiasts who take proper safety precautions and only leave footprints behind them.

I cannot stress too highly the dangers involved with many of the underground works deteriorating. As an added precaution I have refrained from revealing the exact location of entrances wherever possible. Please be content with reading about them in this book and, possibly, looking at the websites mentioned in my sources.

Derek Leach

Introduction

Set in a valley between chalk cliffs formed 136 million years ago when submerged under deep water, the Dover area is riddled with caves and tunnels constructed over many centuries, often for military purposes but also for civilian use as: storage, dwellings, shelters and industry such as a foundry and mushroom growing – not to mention smuggling! Dover's caves and tunnels, both old and new, played an important part in both world wars. Most of them were used to protect civilians or the military.

In such a strategic position only 20 miles from the continent, Dover has been under threat of attack for centuries, but always from the sea. The 20th century saw a completely new threat from the air. The first bomb to be dropped on Great Britain fell in Dover on Christmas Eve 1914. The existing protection on all sides was made obsolete by bombs and shells. During the Second World War, Dover's population was closer to the front line than anywhere else in Britain. Nowhere else could civilians see German troops on the French coast with long range guns able to bombard Dover. No other town suffered so long.

People have used caves and dug deep from prehistoric days to the present day to preserve themselves. By going underground people could be safe from attack. Times and needs change. What was once a sophisticated defence system becomes obsolete and disused. Excavations so laboriously made are abandoned and forgotten with nature soon covering all trace, but underground they still exist, deteriorating and potentially dangerous to those who might explore them.

This book attempts to describe most of the caves and tunnels in the Dover area, their uses and people's memories of them. They, too, are part and parcel of Dover's incredible heritage and deserve to be honoured in this humble way.

PART ONE
MILITARY PURPOSES

Chapter 1
Dover Castle

The story of Dover's caves and tunnels must begin with the great, stone fortress and royal residence of Dover Castle commenced by Henry II in 1180, which has defended the gateway to England ever since, albeit modernised frequently over the centuries to keep pace with military needs. Underground works at the castle have played an important role from earliest times through to the 20th century when they became more important than the buildings above ground.

(Pic. 1) Dover Castle

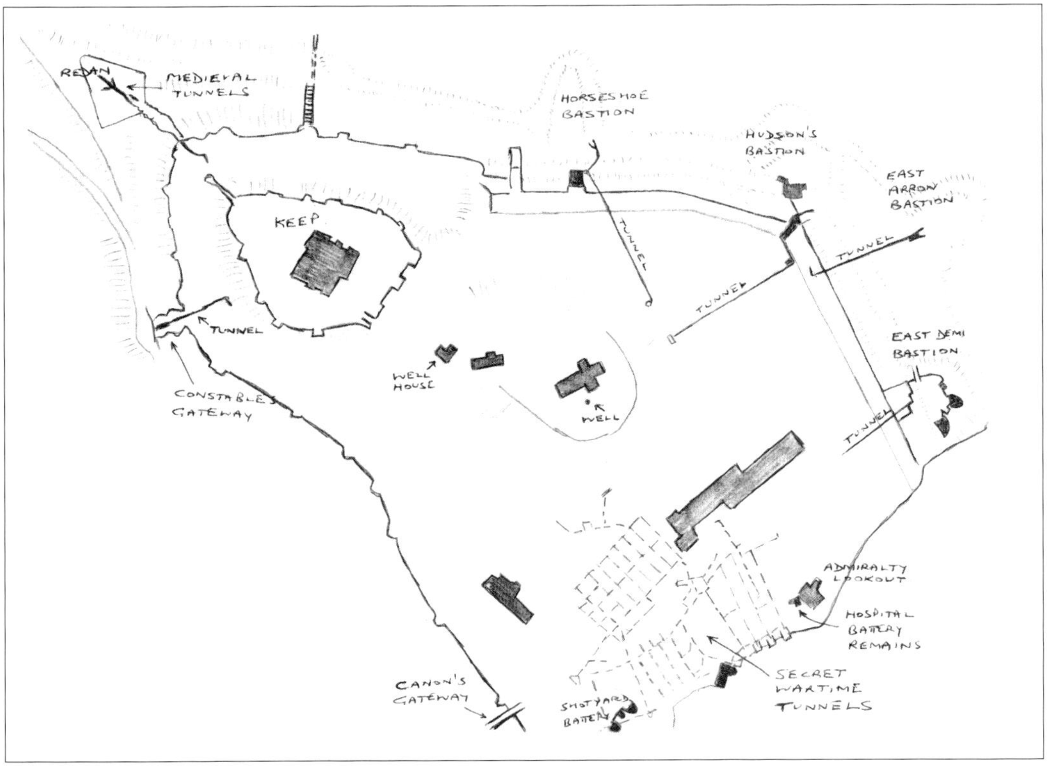

(Pic. 2) Castle sketch showing main tunnels

Wells

Mention must be made of the extraordinary well shafts of differing dates that exist in the castle site. As with all strongholds a source of water, particularly for times of siege, was essential. Dover was no exception. On the second floor of the great keep is a chamber where the well shaft can still be seen. The water table is 400 feet (122m) below the keep and the first 172 feet (52m) of the shaft are lined with Caen stone and the remainder natural chalk. In the 1790s another well which survives was dug on Palace Green. Brick-lined it is about 280 feet (84m) deep and 10 feet (3m) across, incorporating an iron staircase. A steam-driven winch pulled up the water. Many visitors pass the Well House today without realising what lies beneath. Yet another well thought to be of Saxon origin is situated on the mound beside the church of St. Mary-in-Castro. It is about 320 feet (96m) deep and lined with stone and flint until it passes through the earth mound into solid chalk. Any Saxon settlement around

(Pic. 3) Castle keep well

this ancient church would have needed a source of water. The historian Hasted stated that in 1066 King Harold offered to William of Normandy 'the castle of Dover with the well of water in it.' This was, of course, well before the stone keep was built and almost certainly refers to the well by the church.

The siege of 1216

Not only the English or Brits tunnelled in Dover; the French did too! Following the construction of Dover Castle in the late 12th century, it came under siege from the French in 1216. King John had left the defence of the castle in the capable hands of Hubert de Burgh, Justiciar of England (the chief political and legal officer in the land), whilst the French were commanded by Louis, the French Dauphin. Concentrating his attack on the north gateway, Louis's men, out of sight of the defenders, burrowed into the chalk and undermined the timber defences of the barbican. Coupled with the damage caused by the French siege engines, the outer defences crumbled and the defenders withdrew behind the main stone walls. Once again the French tunnelled into the chalk and undermined the eastern gate tower. The defenders may well have guessed what was happening as there are small tunnels from within the castle which may have been dug in the hope of breaking into the French tunnel. If so, they were unsuccessful. The French tunnel was mined and the gate tower collapsed, allowing the French to pour through. After fierce fighting the French were driven off.

The siege demonstrated that the castle was not impregnable. This had to be remedied. Construction work over the next 40 years transformed the castle and included elaborate tunnels that are probably unique in English medieval fortifications. These gave the castle garrison when attacked the ability to 'sally forth' and surprise the enemy – something lacking in 1216.

(Pic. 4) 13th century tunnel to northern spur

Spur tunnels

A substantial northern outwork called, because of its shape, the spur (ie a sharp projection) or redan (a V-shaped salient or projection toward an expected attack) was built beyond the castle ditch. From the castle a tunnel under the old north gateway (Norfolk Towers of today) was excavated, leading to a short, roofed passage into the new St. John's Tower sited in the ditch. A drawbridge on the north side of the tower led to another short tunnel within the spur. A 1737 survey shows what is thought to be original 13th century work – vaulted chambers and passageways that still exist behind the later brickwork.

Although mainly abandoned by the 16th

(Pic. 5) Spur tunnels 1804 caponiers

century, this link survived partially until the 18th century. In the 1750s the underground passage became exposed when the moat was deepened and the passage was given a brick roof. Faced with the threat from France in the 1790s, the castle was strengthened, including the modernisation of the medieval spur. Lieutenant Colonel Twiss of the Royal Engineers carried out the changes. Spiral stairs were constructed to new brick-lined tunnels connected to the steeply sloping passage dug in the early 13th century. Further down this ancient passage, it cuts through, at a slightly higher level, a rough tunnel at right angles. This may well be one of the tunnels dug by the defenders in 1216 to intercept and destroy the enemy's mining tunnels. In the main passage is a grating covering a shaft to an even deeper early 19th century tunnel, providing a lower tier of communication to the outer defences. It also enabled the possible mining, if necessary, of the Deal Road. Eventually the medieval tunnel, having emerged from the castle bank, goes into a short covered passage until the post 1216 St. John's Tower is reached in the middle of the moat. On the far side of the tower Twiss constructed in 1804 two storey brick caponiers (ie covered passages within a ditch allowing sweeping fire along the ditch), which allowed defenders to cover the moat with guns. The only way into the spur from the castle is via a timber stairway in St. John's Tower to the lower level of caponier at the end of which is a spiral staircase up to the northern section of the medieval tunnels within the spur. Here the 1230 tunnel divided into three passages, two of which are now blocked, but originally continued upwards giving access to all parts of the spur. The one that survives was adapted to link with Napoleonic guardrooms protecting a doorway leading to the rear of the spur. In 1853 two short caponiers were constructed jutting out from the passage north of St. John's Tower with passages from their end to galleries in the outer wall of the redan's moat. The tunnels were enlarged and further modernised at this time, which is what exists today.

Fitzwilliam's Gate

The construction of Fitzwilliam's Gate in the NE exterior wall of the castle was another post 1216 strengthening, enabling defenders to sally forth on the east side. R. A. Brown in his book *Dover Castle* states that references to work on an underground gate first appear in 1227 and references to the digging of tunnels in 1230. In 1229 £100 was spent on making a tunnel or vault to 'go out of the castle towards the field', possibly a reference to the medieval tunnels at Fitzwilliam's Gate commenced in 1227. It guarded an underground passage originally carried over the moat by a covered bridge and then through the outer bank to a gateway from which defenders could emerge unseen to attack the enemy from the rear.

(Pic. 6) Fitzwilliam's Gate medieval tunnel

Constable's Tower

In 1233 the King ordered that arches be made at the entrance and exit of the tunnels of Dover Castle and in 1234 two new towers were made at the exit of the 'new Tunnel'. Also in 1234 another tunnel was being covered with lead. These could refer to Constable's Tower and gateway, built between 1221 and 1227 to replace the blocked northern gateway, where a tunnel was

(Pic. 7) 13th century Constable's Tower and Gateway

excavated from the keep mound to emerge below the drawbridge of Constable's Tower gateway, allowing fire upwards to catch attackers on the drawbridge or to sortie into the dry moat. By 1256 major construction work at the castle ceased until Henry VIII's reign.

Napoleonic period

War with France broke out in 1793, but an invasion from France was not a real threat until 1803 when Napoleon's main aim was to defeat Great Britain. Lieutenant Colonel William Twiss, a very able military engineer, was in charge of military works at Dover from 1792 to 1809. The castle's defences were substantially strengthened with most effort going into its vulnerable eastern side. Here four strong, earthen outworks were built beyond the main defences and the outer bank: the massive Horseshoe Bastion, (just east of Avranches Tower) Hudson's Bastion (to the south-east), East Demi-Bastion (at the cliff edge) and East Arrow Bastion (detached and on the slope between Hudson's and East Demi bastions). Whilst the first three were accessed by their own underground passages from far behind the main rampart and with doorways protected by drawbridges into the moat, East Arrow Bastion's passage led into the moat. The tunnel to Horseshoe Bastion reaches a substantial vaulted chamber after about 300 feet (90m), probably for use in peacetime

(Pic. 8) Hudson's Bastion

(Pic. 9) Ditch entrance to East Arrow Bastion tunnel

(Pic. 10) Tunnel to East Demi Bastion

(Pic. 11) Caponier entrances in Canon's Gateway

as bomb proof living accommodation for 45 men or 150 during a siege, before continuing another 75 feet (22.5m) to the Bastion. The tunnel entrance is at the foot of the church mound, whilst another entrance close by gives access to Hudson's Passage. Before going under the rampart a spiral staircase provides an alternative entrance. Upon reaching the NE ditch, communication is through a caponier to Hudson's Bastion itself. East Arrow Bastion was a detached work and its 225 feet (67m) long communicating tunnel started in the bottom of the main NE ditch rather than inside the castle walls. The shortest bastion tunnel, 180 feet (53m), is that to East Demi-Bastion accessed close to the 1856 Officers' Barracks. Gun galleries were also built into the walls of the moat at this time, which were linked by passages to enable troops to move between them unseen.

The construction by Twiss of Canon's Gate and its protection included a small tunnel under the outer bank of the medieval moat to a vertical brick shaft behind the new outer rampart. This enabled soldiers to reach the outer defences without exposing themselves to enemy fire. Two entrances in the gateway provide access to the three levels of the caponier below with their rifle slits commanding the moat. Revd. J. Lyon, a local historian writing in 1814, when describing the construction of the new gate included: 'In sinking the ground within the castle to level it with the new road, the workmen came to a souterrain, excavated out of the solid rock, several feet under the present surface; but the use for which it was originally intended, is now very uncertain.' A souterrain is an excavated cave or tunnel.

(Pics. 12, 13) A Guilford Shaft stairway and tunnel

Guilford Shaft

Guilford Shaft links Henry VIII's Moat's Bulwark, which clings to the lower cliff face, with Dover Castle on the cliffs above. The shaft was begun in 1793 and in February 1795 was still under construction as a report from Lieutenant Bruyeres describes the arrangements for sinking a third shaft between the castle and Moat's Bulwark. This is because Guilford Shaft is in fact four shafts with 214 steps in total linked by tunnels. These tunnels were lighting passages onto the cliff face and had doors with firing slits for defence against an attack up the shaft. Revd J. Lyon wrote: 'Near the edge of the cliff, and not far from the end of the wall, a shaft has been sunk, one hundred and ninety feet deep, to form a communication with Moat's Bulwark, which was built at the foot of the cliff by Henry VIII. In this shaft there are circular stairs; and when the Prince of Wales visited the Castle, in the year 1798 he was conducted down it, as the nearest way to the town.' During the Second World War the connecting passages were lined with corrugated steel and appear to have become observation posts with new accommodation tunnels added behind them.

(Pic. 14) Moat's Bulwark

Original Casemate Level

Most of the tunnels in the castle cliff known today as Casemate Level were dug at the end of the 18th century – a casemate being a vaulted chamber in a fortress. Needing to house many more troops in the castle, a radical solution was begun in 1797 when Royal Engineers (REs) tunnellers excavated inwards from the cliff face to provide extraordinary underground accommodation – safe from warship bombardment

(Pic. 15) Alternative Napoleonic entrance to Casemate level

and from any landward artillery. Four parallel tunnels 100 feet (30m) long with ventilation shafts were dug first for soldiers' accommodation followed by three larger and longer tunnels for officers, all connected by a linking tunnel. Between them a fresh water well and latrines were built. This well shaft can still be seen via a simple tunnel at ground level. It is supported in part now by steel rings with corrugated shuttering, partly brick-lined and the remainder rough chalk. From the entrance 50 steps down lead to a 190 feet (57m) long tunnel which ends with a 12 feet (3.6m) diameter vertical chalk shaft running both above to Casemate Level and below the tunnel where water level is reached after 25 feet (7.5m). Casemate waste drains fed into a brick-lined shaft that was tunnelled through the cliff to connect the underground barracks' latrines to the sea.

(Pic. 16) Well shaft and cable tunnel

Access to the whole complex was via an underground ramp near Canon's Gate. At the back of the seven casemated barrack tunnels a second communication passage was constructed, leading to another entrance further from the cliff edge via a double spiral staircase. All the tunnels had fireplaces with flues cut through the chalk and a number of ventilation shafts. The seaward ends of the tunnels had brick fronts with doors and windows. By the end of 1798 the work was finished, but, because of a number of chalk falls, the accommodation tunnels were brick-lined by 1810 and could probably house about 2,000 men plus officers. The first troops moved in during 1803, sleeping in iron bedsteads with kit hung from pegs on the walls.

During this same period the large garrison meant that privies draining into cesspits were inadequate. This problem was solved by connecting the cast-iron toilets to a pipe that carried the waste to the cliff face and down the outside of the cliff.

Disposing of surface water was another logistical problem, which was solved by the construction of elaborate drainage tunnels around the castle, one example being evident in the moat near Hurst's Tower where there is a brick-lined shaft 60 feet (18m) deep and 4 feet (1.25m) across with a tunnel at the bottom.

19th century

With the end of the Napoleonic Wars the rapid reduction in the number of men in the army led to the casemate barracks being abandoned by the military, but they were soon occupied by the Coastal Blockade Service, formed in 1817 to combat smuggling along the South Coast, and were used as their local headquarters until 1828. To improve access to the beach a zig-zag staircase was cut by REs. The tunnels then became a vast ammunition store, but with the end of the Crimean War in 1856 additional military accommodation for returning soldiers was needed and the British Swiss Legion was billeted there. They were the lucky ones as many were housed in tents on the Western Heights!

Another threat from France when ruled by Napoleon III resulted in strengthening and modernising the Dover defences in the 1850s both at the castle and on the Western Heights. These included several new gun batteries at the castle, including the amusingly named Shoulder of Mutton Battery, reached by a tunnel from the SW moat, Saluting Battery and Shot Yard Battery each with their submerged magazines and communicating passages. Access to the Long Gun powder magazine was via a tunnel with an entrance and staircase by the modern ticket office. Apparently Women's Auxiliary Air Force

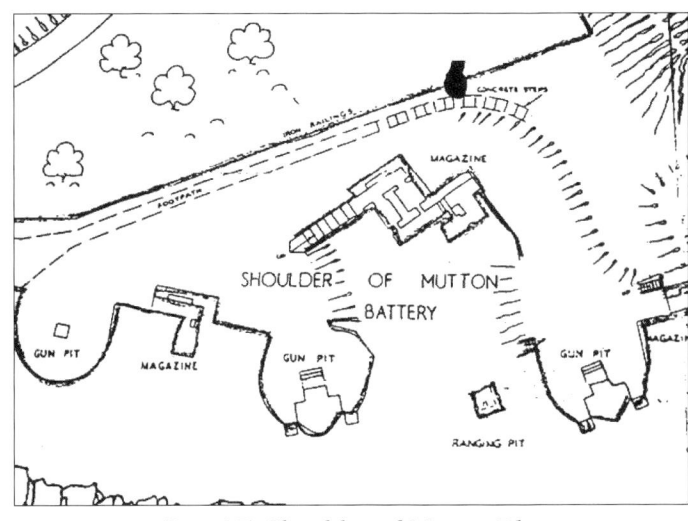

(Pic. 17) Shoulder of Mutton Plan

(WAAFs) staff were billeted in this tunnel during the Second World War. In addition Hospital Battery was constructed on the cliff edge in 1891, although little survives except a powder magazine converted to a storeroom underneath what is now Admiral's Lookout.

Second World War

No extensions to the tunnels were made during the First World War and between 1918 and 1939 the castle tunnels were used by the REs for storage. Following the Munich Crisis, however, with another war looming in the 1930s, a local naval and military headquarters (HQ) was needed; learning from the experience of heavy bombing during the Spanish Civil War, it had to be bomb proof. In 1938 the old Napoleonic tunnels were chosen and modernised. Whilst the original large, brick-lined,

(Pic. 18) Access to Hospital Battery

casemate tunnels were altered, the communications tunnels were left virtually intact. The Royal Navy (RN) moved in during 1939 and occupied the eastern set of tunnels, which were converted to house the essential communications rooms – coding room, wireless office and teleprinter room – to enable the HQ to liaise with the Admiralty, warships at sea, other naval stations as well as the Army and Royal Air Force (RAF). At the seaward end of one tunnel the Flag Officer Dover, Vice Admiral Bertram Ramsay, had his private quarters with views over the Channel to the French coast. The western set was occupied by the Garrison Commander, the Coastal Artillery operations room and the anti-aircraft (AA) operations room. The remainder was used for storage and dormitories, although even these were later converted to offices. No sleeping accommodation was provided underground, except for the Admiral! Underground, German speaking staff listened in to enemy transmissions as well as sending false messages to cause confusion! The new masts at Swingate, part of the world's first radar chain, gave early warning of German air activity. A naval telephone exchange was built in the tunnels between 1939 and 1941 and a pneumatic tube system carried messages between the tunnels and the rest of the castle.

It was in these tunnels 50 feet (15m) below the cliff top, known as Casemate Level, that Vice Admiral Bertram Ramsay and his staff planned and carried out, under code name Operation Dynamo, the miraculous evacuation of 338,000 British, French and Belgian troops from Dunkirk during nine days commencing 26 May 1940. Exhausted personnel, working around the clock, snatched a few minutes sleep on chairs whenever they could.

It is widely believed that the code name for the Dunkirk evacuation, Operation Dynamo, was chosen locally and named after a generating (dynamo) room in the castle tunnels. This cannot be true, however, since the dynamo room was not built until 1942. The code name Operation Dynamo was in fact chosen by the Admiralty (there is an Admiralty signal to that effect dated 22 May 1940). It was for this reason, therefore, that the planning room for the evacuation became known as the Dynamo Room.

After Dunkirk and the imminent threat of invasion, Dover's defences were strengthened. As the expected focus for any invasion Dover became the best protected part of the coastline.

More underground work was also needed. 172 Tunnelling Company arrived in East Kent in November 1940 with 6 projects: to excavate for five air raid shelters for coastal artillery (at St. Margaret's Bay, St. Margaret's at Cliffe, Fan Bay, Western Heights Beach Defence Battery and Lydden Spout) as well as for extra underground accommodation at the castle. Beginning in early 1941 the castle tunnels were extended by three military tunnelling companies. More communications equipment required another tunnel next to the eastern tunnels, which was used by the General Post Office (GPO) for batteries and charging equipment for the telephone and teleprinter networks. This was located to the west of the 18th century officers' tunnels. A new passage was dug between Admiralty casemate and the casemate shared by Coastal Artillery HQ and the AA operations room as well as a new telephone exchange, linking the original communications tunnel directly with the operations room.

Hellfire Corner Casemate level
(not to scale)

(Pic. 19) Plan of WW2 Casemate level

(Pic. 20) Casemate accommodation

(Pic. 21) Casemate plotting room

Annexe Level

A completely new set of tunnels on a grid pattern was dug above and to the west of Casemate Level, called Annexe. With men working around the clock in shifts for 5 months they were completed in January 1942, although not fitted out until the autumn. Compared with the lofty, spacious, brick-lined tunnels of the 1790s Casemate Level, the tunnels of Annexe set out in a grid pattern were cramped and steel-lined. They were intended as a medical dressing station to provide first aid for battle casualties on the British mainland if invaded. Fortunately, it was never used for that purpose; instead, throughout the war it was used as the castle garrison's medical centre complete with surgeons, nurses, orderlies and cooks. With far fewer casualties than expected, Annexe also provided overflow sleeping accommodation and messing facilities for the Combined HQ (CHQ).

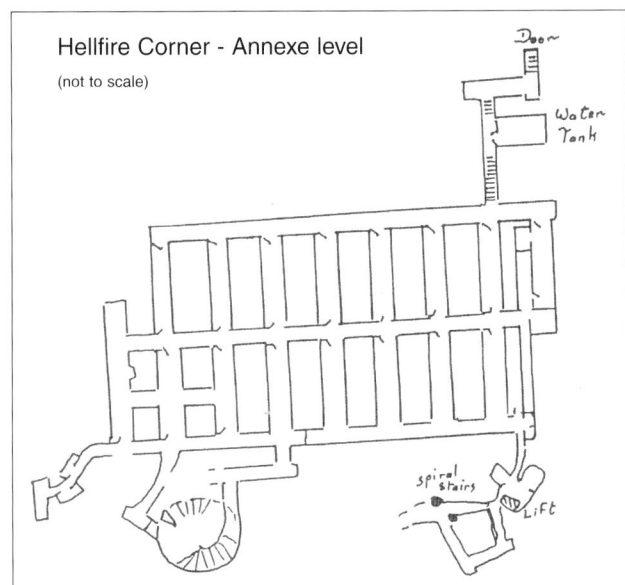

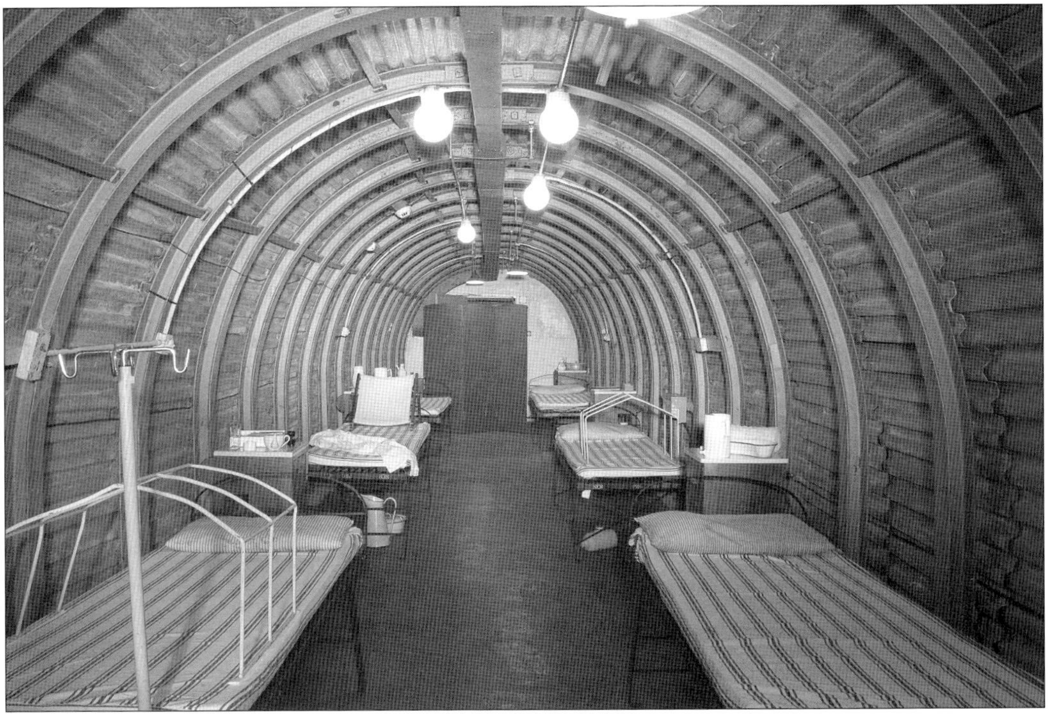

(Pic. 22) Plan of WW2 Annexe level

(Pic. 23) Annexe level accommodation

Disposal of the chalk spoil presented a problem. At first it was dumped over the castle cliff edge, but there were soon complaints from property owners below and steps were taken to protect the properties from falling chalk. The actual tunnelling was, of course, dangerous work – a rock fall at Capel in 1941 killed 2 REs.

Mysterious Bastion Level

There is considerable controversy and mystery about another level of tunnels called Bastion and whether the excavations were ever started or partially completed but abandoned. Dr. Semple in his thesis of 2005 concluded that Bastion was probably planned but never carried out. He states that in August 1942 planning began on a new project for a CHQ to be built on a new level called Bastion and that if it was ever partially built, it must have been between completion of Annexe Level and the start of work on Dumpy level – the eventual site for the CHQ. Dr. Semple's research, however, found no record of any such work in the first half of 1941 (either at the Public Record Office or the RE Museum Chatham). Plans for the CHQ were not made until the summer of 1942. Bastion was intended either as additional accommodation, since both the Army and Navy were looking for safer accommodation for female staff, or a CHQ. Bastion Level would have been only a few feet higher than Casemate Level.

On the other hand Jonathan Coad, author of a book on Dover Castle published in 1995, states that in late 1941 work began on yet another new level called Bastion to house a CHQ for the Army, RN and RAF in readiness for the planned invasion of Europe. It was to comprise a central operations room with offices and communications equipment and a short tunnel leading to Casemate. Apparently to the east of the spiral staircase a new passage was excavated parallel to the rear communication passage as well as a spur tunnel running eastwards from the head of the eastern (Admiralty) tunnel. These were intended to provide access to Bastion level without disrupting the work of the existing headquarters, but as Bastion level was never completed these tunnels lead nowhere. Mr Coad asserts that following dangerous rock falls and subsidence, the partially completed level was abandoned.

Prior to 2000 little was known about Bastion Level, but a former RE sergeant major, Mr Groves, who was stationed at the castle during the war, wrote to Jonathan Coad of English Heritage (EH) offering information. Apparently, Mr Groves had written a book about the tunnels between 1965 and 1970 but the Ministry of Defence had refused permission to publish as the secret Regional Seat of Government, based in the complex, was still in use. His manuscript contained useful information about this level called Bastion. According to Mr Groves it suffered a major collapse when partly excavated and was abandoned and sealed in 1941. Mr Groves claimed that this was kept secret to spare the government the embarrassment of an expensive mistake. He made a final inspection of Bastion in 1958, gaining access from Casemate Level by crawling through a cable tunnel, the only connection with Casemate.

Mr Groves stated that entry for construction was via a tunnel from the wall of the moat in the NE ditch. This access was sealed in 1958 and the moat wall reinstated. Additional evidence came from a Miss Thomas in 1996 who said that she had worked in the underground operations room, gaining access from the eastern side through a gate and then into a tunnel leading to the operations room. She was able to describe the walk through East

Demi Passage and into a tunnel from NE Ditch to Bastion Level.

Only one plan was known to exist, but attempts by EH to locate Bastion using bore holes failed. Then in 2000 EH commissioned Graham Daws Associates to find Bastion at about 205 feet (62.5m). The access tunnel in the NE ditch was found, brick-lined and 5 feet (1.45m) wide but packed with chalk and rammed with clay as described by Mr Groves. A second parallel tunnel was also found about three feet away, but probably not of Second World War origin, rather the same period as the ditch wall. Radar surveys indicated the existence of a telephone exchange at Bastion Level. A small shaft was sunk but nothing was found. Neither was the cable tunnel found that Mr Groves had used in 1958. The investigation concluded that there was no trace of Bastion, but its existence could not be ruled out because of Mr Groves' manuscript. It was possible that the plan of Bastion, regarding its location, was not accurate. Mr Groves also claimed that there were plans to build two more levels.

Dumpy

Bastion, real or imagined, was replaced by another new level 50 feet (16m) below Casemate. Dumpy, as it was eventually called, needed steep staircases to connect with Casemate. This level for CHQ was completed in 9 months (August 1942 – April 1943) and was occupied during the summer of 1943, but the navy and coastal artillery stayed put in Casemate to concentrate on defending the Dover Strait. The RAF moved its operations centre (for air-sea rescue and air support) from nearby Swingate into the new CHQ, probably as the result of the Channel Dash fiasco. (This was the daring successful dash of the German warships *Scharnhorst*, *Gneisenau* and *Prinz Eugen* on 12 February 1942 through the Dover Strait, escaping coastal shelling, air attacks and British destroyers). For some reason, existing staff both male and female were reluctant to move into the new level. This CHQ would have masterminded the invasion of Europe if the Calais area had been chosen, but the Normandy landings meant that a similar CHQ at Portsmouth was used.

The incredible resources of money and manpower spent on these works demonstrate their importance at the time. From the top level down, the four known levels of tunnels in the cliffs of Dover Castle are; Annexe (235 feet or 71.6m above sea level), Casemate 194 feet or 59m), Dumpy (144 feet or 43.9m) and Esplanade, which subdivides into Drainage Tunnels (70 feet or 21.3m) and the Cable/Well Tunnel (22 feet or 6.7m). The Well Tunnel goes up through Dumpy Level and terminates at Casemate.

Whilst within the castle grounds there is a mile of

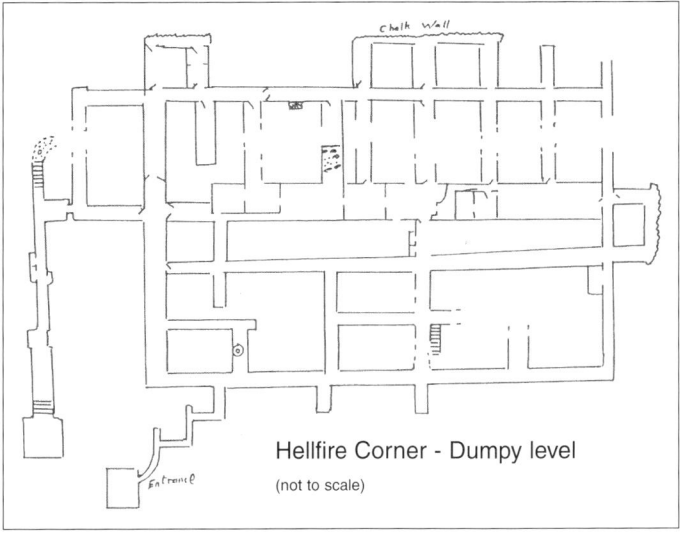

(Pic. 24) Plan of WW2 Dumpy level

16

medieval tunnels and two miles of Napoleonic tunnels, the 20th century added another 4 or 5 miles.

Between Dunkirk in 1940 and D-Day in 1944 the amount of military tunnelling work was unprecedented in Britain, dwarfing the Napoleonic efforts. The provision of safe underground communications centres and combined operational headquarters were a priority. Dover's underground military accommodation was probably the most extensive provided anywhere in Britain. For most of the war the Dover area was a fortress, being continually extended and improved with much of it underground, which could be besieged at any time by the enemy.

Uniquely, Dover was categorised as an active service sector of the Army. Troops stationed in Dover were the only soldiers in Britain classified as being on active service. This recognised the dangers from bombing and shelling for the military. The danger was, of course, just as real for the people of Dover. Military casualties in Dover were, however, remarkably light compared with civilians and the castle was only hit occasionally by shells.

Working conditions in the castle tunnels were not good with little opportunity to see sunlight. A sunlight clinic was considered in 1942 to counter depression and by 1944 sun beds were provided for the female staff. Presumably men had no such needs!

Q Dover

The Defence Telegraph Network (DTN), later called Q, and operated by GPO engineers, was conceived in 1938 to provide a communications network for the Navy and RAF separate from the public telephone network, including the distribution in code of weather information.

(Pic. 25) Telecommunications equipment

The DTN equipment was installed in the castle tunnels in 1941 and removed in 1974 following the closure of Q Dover. It occupied two of the main casemates with one housing the generators and batteries for power and the other the telecommunications equipment. There were also two smaller linked tunnels housing the Military and Combined Services telephone exchange. GPO telephone engineers were stationed there around the clock in 12 hour shifts throughout the war to maintain the system. In addition to all this equipment the engineers had to maintain and repair the equipment in the operational rooms. There was an AA Control Room, plotting rooms for the Navy and RAF, apparatus room with special keyboards for the plotting rooms, 120 teleprinters, Military and Combined Services Exchange, Naval Private Manual Exchange, numerous radio monitoring units and seven miles of pneumatic message tubing. The top of the Roman Pharos housed a Navy transmitter. Further eastwards was Naval HQ and operations centre, then the Army operations room commanding the coastal and cross Channel guns. Furthest east was the Dynamo Room. There was also a 12 position telephone exchange, manned by female staff from the Women's Royal Naval Service (WRNS), Auxiliary Territorial Service (ATS) and the WAAF, as well as the Post Office telephone network. WAAFs also manned the air/sea rescue section that received messages about allied and enemy airmen in the sea, plotted their positions and sent out rescue craft.

According to Charles Hutchins, Dumpy comprised: a plotting room and a radio room for each service, a main signals office, many small offices, teleprinter room with 20 machines staffed by WAAFs and a much larger teleprinter room with 60 or 70 machines manned by women from all three services. There were three DTN engineers per shift plus female assistants responsible for fault reporting and recording.

In preparation for the invasion of Europe in 1943, the Post Office ran its submarine cables from the complex down the Napoleonic well through the cliffs to an access tunnel emerging at East Cliff ready to be laid across the Channel when the time came after D-Day.

Post war

After the war some of the communications equipment remained in use and had to be maintained as the RN kept an interest in the cliff tunnels, but even they moved out in 1958. During the Cold War and the threat of nuclear war with Russia, the Home Office took over the complex as a ready-made site, safe from nuclear attack and radioactive fallout, for one of ten Regional Seats of Government (RSG), which were to function if a nuclear attack destroyed the national government in London. It would have housed for several weeks about 270 essential staff drawn from the county council as well as water and telecommunications engineers. Dumpy Level was mainly used with substantial sums spent on a lift to connect all three levels with the cliff top and new communications equipment, a modern ventilation system, generators and large reserves of fuel, food and water. The fully self-contained RSG, including control rooms, communications equipment rooms, air filtering machinery, generators, oil storage tanks, food store, water supplies, living quarters and even a BBC studio, would be able to survive for a period without external access, connected by telephone to other RSGs and the Home Office control centre.

On Casemate Level all the old wartime equipment was removed and the eastern tunnel abandoned whilst the western tunnels were converted to dormitories and canteens. The RSG was abandoned in 1984 and the equipment removed. Casemate Level was opened to the public in 1990 by English Heritage who, by then, had taken over Dover Castle from the military.

Q Dover staff memories

The GPO engineers, stationed in the castle tunnels as part of Q Dover, started holding reunion dinners after the war, which still continue, although numbers are inevitably dwindling. Their memories were recounted in a book on Q Dover produced by Stuart Hall. Mr Nye remembered being called out at all hours because messages were not getting through the pneumatic tube system only to find, after dismantling sections of tube, that the culprit was an apple or something similar. Roy Hooker remembered frantic activity to smarten up the place before Prime Minister Winston Churchill arrived. King George VI also visited; Ken De Coster, busy clearing a message tube, missed a lightning tour by Field Marshal Montgomery. One of George Shepherd's first impressions was 'WRNS at every turn!' It took him several days to find his way around, going into a toilet block only to find a female coming out of the next cubicle! The engineers were encouraged to stock up their lockers with emergency rations in case they had to stay over because of bombing or shelling. It happened, sleeping wherever they could. A welcome surprise was fluorescent lighting in all the offices and work places, which was completely new in 1943.

Charles Hutchins was on duty in 1944 when Royal Marines from Deal tested the defences. They managed to find a tiny entrance tunnel on the cliffside and 'went through CHQ like the proverbial dose of salts!' The thunderflashes that were set off were deafening.

The tunnels were reputed to have ghosts and there were various strange happenings: 'The Headless Drummer was the most difficult to deal with – the mess he made when offered a cup of tea!' said Peter Wall. Perhaps they could be explained, however, by rats in the corridors, wind lifting the lino on the floor or wind blowing through the tunnels. With rats and mice exploring the tunnels a station cat was recruited and named Toscanini. Tosca for short preferred better food and would steal anything, including a large, beef joint at Christmas.

Peter Wall recalled that GPO engineers had to be on hand to repair faults quickly, but there was also lots of routine maintenance to keep the system running smoothly. There were also some quiet periods when hobbies such as building radio sets could be pursued or the time could be used profitably to study for additional qualifications. Mealbreaks might include a game of darts. The annual reunions after the war were held in the retiring room at Q Dover so that those on duty could join in, but after the closure of the repeater station in 1974 the annual dinner became lunch at a pub.

Peter Pennington was subject to an initiation ceremony when he joined in 1962. After being given a guided tour of Casemate Level he was taken down to Dumpy, but then was left to study a wall map of the Dumpy layout. 'There was a distant clunk noise and all the lights went out. I had never seen, if that's the right word, such total darkness before. I learnt an important lesson – never be without a torch in Dumpy in case there was another power failure, man made or otherwise!' He was set up again when told to go into a dark tunnel with a dim torch to mend a teleprinter: 'In the poor light I saw the body of a soldier. An old army uniform had been stuffed with rags and topped with a tin hat!' Peter also recalls weekend exercises being held in the RSG period. Girls from the Dover telephone exchange were drafted in to man the exchange backed up by GPO engineers. The girls used the GPO rest room for their breaks and so 'girlie' pictures had to be removed before they arrived. 'As "tea boy" I opened a cupboard to get out cups and saucers for the girls. Shock! Horror! The inside of the cupboard door was still covered with "girlie" pictures. I tried to shield them from view, but was too late – the girls took offence and stormed out. And this was in the swinging sixties!'

Ghosts

Dover Castle boasts several ghosts and it seems that its tunnels are no exception. Since they have been opened to the public there have been several 'sightings'. One visitor tells how during a guided tour he saw a soldier in a Second World War uniform standing against a wall, holding what looked like a clipboard. They looked at each other and then the soldier turned round and disappeared through a dead end wall! Nobody else, it seemed, had looked down that passage and seen the soldier. Another visitor tried to take a photograph in the tunnels but the flash did not work. Later, however, she looked at the images she had taken which included the 'failed' photograph that showed strange, transparent legs and what looked like a face above them with yet another face at the top of the picture. On another occasion while listening to a tour guide 10 people apparently heard a cat cry several times. Whilst walking down a spiral staircase a girl could smell flowers, but her boyfriend could smell nothing. When they reached the bottom the smell had gone. Walking through the tunnels, once again the girl could smell flowers. She stopped walking and looked behind her; deadly pale, she said that she had seen a woman carrying a bunch of freshly-cut flowers coming towards them and walking right through them, shaking dew off the flowers as she went! Her back felt a bit wet and the boyfriend confirmed that there were three small splashes, but he smelt and saw nothing.

Chapter 2
Western Heights

It is impossible to describe sensibly the underground works on the Western Heights without briefly setting them in their context. Following the outbreak of war in 1775 with the American colonies that were supported by the French, steps were taken not only to strengthen the castle's defences but also to fortify the heights to the west of the town. Whilst construction work began in the 1770s, the two main building phases of this incredible fortress were 1804-16 and 1858-67. Eventually, it comprised three independent forts – the Citadel, North Centre Bastion and Drop Redoubt – linked by a series of defensive ditches and banks. This simple description conceals an incredibly complex, impregnable fortress, honeycombed with casemates, gun rooms, underground galleries, passages and stair shafts. In many cases it is difficult to decide whether or not a particular feature can be regarded as a tunnel or not!

(Pic. 26) Aerial view of the Western Heights

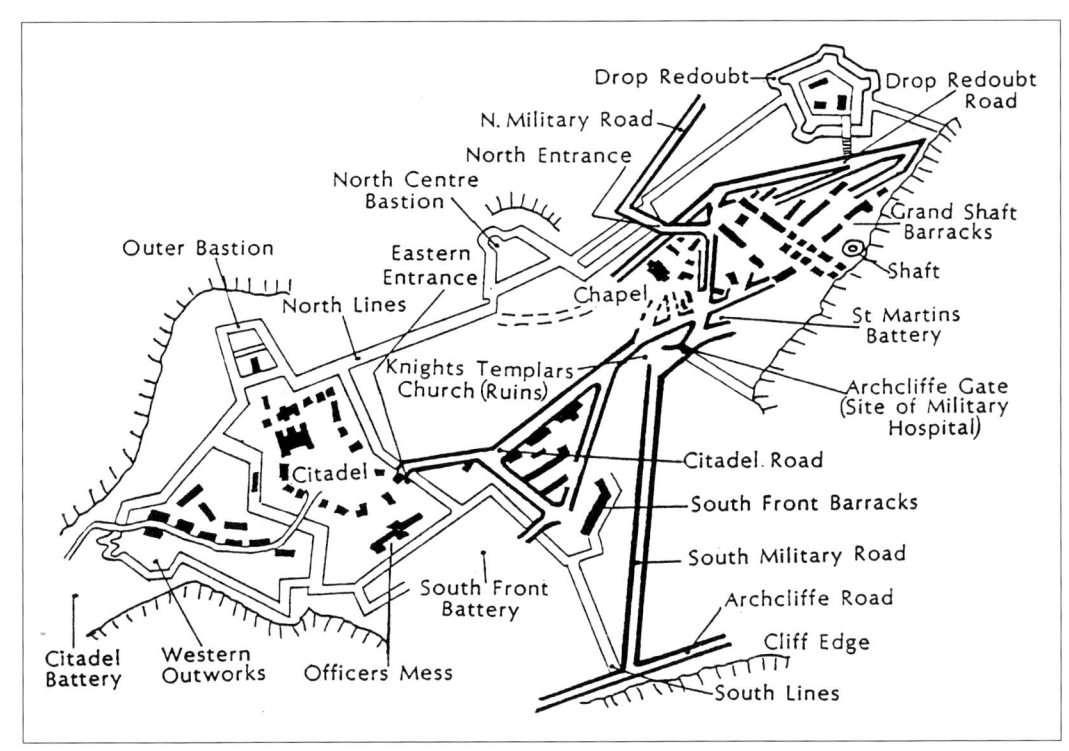

(Pic. 27) Western Heights plan

(Pic. 28) Drop Redoubt

(Pic. 29) Drop Redoubt caponier

(Pic. 30) Drop Redoubt caponier

No attack was expected from the sea below; the fort's primary function was to conceal a base from which a French army, having landed elsewhere, could be attacked from the rear. Since the fortress is largely buried in the hilltop, it is invisible from a distance unlike the prominent medieval castle on the east cliff.

By 1770 there were temporary, small earthworks for infantry and artillery. Grander plans were made and a substantial fortification was begun by 1782, but with the war over in 1783, construction work halted only to recommence with even bigger projects during the wars with the new French republic and then Napoleon from 1793 to 1815. Revised plans of 1804 linked the Drop Redoubt site and the Citadel site by earthworks. When work stopped once more in 1815, following the defeat of Napoleon, only the Drop Redoubt, begun in 1782, was complete. This pentagonal fort was surrounded by a deep ditch and comprised four casemated soldiers' quarters, officers' quarters, privies and ablutions plus a large magazine. Caponiers were added in 1858-67each linked by a tunnel to the centre of the redoubt. The entrance was via a bridge over the ditch and a tunnel through the rampart.

Grand Shaft

New works in 1803 included accommodation for 700 men in barracks (Grand Shaft Barracks) and 800 in casemate accommodation within the fortress. The need, however, to move troops quickly from this safe position to other sites under attack at sea level posed a problem. Whilst the barracks were only 180 feet (54m) above sea level, the route on horseback was almost one and a half miles and on foot, using steep and dangerous footpaths, about three quarters of a mile. Lieutenant Colonel William Twiss RE came up with an ingenious, underground solution: a circular shaft cut into the chalk 26 feet (7.9m) in diameter

(Pic. 31) Grand Shaft bird's eye view

and 140 feet (42.6m) deep. At the bottom of the shaft would be a 180 feet (54.8m) horizontal tunnel to Snargate Street. Started in 1805 and in use by 18F07, the shaft was in fact two brick cylinders, one inside the other. The inner cylinder was pierced by openings to the central light well. Within the brick cylinders are three concentric spiral staircases each with 140 steps. It is said that (except in a war emergency presumably) the staircases were designated: 'Officers and Their Ladies, 'Sergeants and Their Wives' and 'Soldiers and Their Women'. Any such rule was ignored when, later, a Mr Leith from Walmer is said to have ridden a horse up the staircase to win a bet. This incredible Grand Shaft staircase survives to this day, a remarkable tribute to Twiss and his REs.

(Pic. 32) Well house shaft

Citadel

Another engineering feat, a smaller version of the Grand Shaft, was under construction at the same time, but for an entirely different purpose. A well, 440 feet (135.6m) deep, was dug for use in times of siege in the new Citadel fortress, comprising a central brick shaft with two winding staircases for maintenance purposes.

Access to two groups of six gunrooms, known as the Gorge Casemates is via a stair shaft cut through chalk lined with brick; within are two independent staircases around a circular shaft with one leading to the north gunrooms and the other to the south group and the Well House of the 1860s (later the Boiler and Pump House). The Well House survives, comprising two large sunken chambers. A set of four stair shafts descend from the inner NW bastion to underground galleries to

(Pic. 33) Gorge Casemate stairway

provide access to several groups of casemates and expense magazines (ie stores of readily-available ammunition).

A vaulted tunnel through the rampart formed the main entrance to the Citadel and contained a large vaulted chamber, complete with guardroom and cells, which was used to inspect traffic between the inner and outer gateways.

An incredible brick-lined drain tunnel for the Citadel over 1200 feet long and 4? feet high survives.

The Western Outworks, dating from the 1860s, were reached via a long staircase descending in a gallery from the parade ground. A tunnel from the outworks emerges in the South Front Casemates. There is also a drain tunnel from South Casemates to the North Casemates.

Entrances to the fortress

From 1815 there were two main entrances: the South Lines bridge where Old Folkestone Road entered the fortress and the North Entrance on North Military Road. Archcliffe Gate was added in the 1860s (demolished 1963), replacing the original South Entrance.

North Entrance

The North Entrance with bridges over two ditches then went through a tunnel under the rampart of the Lines. This semi-circular, vaulted tunnel with its

(Pic. 34) Citadel drain tunnel

(Pic. 35) Citadel main entrance

(Pic. 36) North entrance stairway

(Pic. 37) North entrance passageway

(Pic. 38) Archcliffe Gate gun rooms

twists and turns to counter any ricochet had a wood block floor to deaden the noise of horses' hooves. A descending stair passage gives on to a brick-vaulted chamber serving a musketry gallery of five vaulted casemates linked by inter-connecting passages plus three gun rooms connected by passages. Steps in the entrance tunnel lead down to a gallery opening into three huge, sunken, water tanks. A rough-hewn passage cut into the chalk from one end of the gallery goes down steeply to connect with the main pipe gallery below Centre Road, which was probably a maintenance access passage. The inner entrance included a casemated guardhouse.

Archcliffe Gate

The impressive Archcliffe Gate had gun rooms, guardhouses and prisoners' cells under the rampart, but most were demolished in 1964 and only the gun rooms

(Pic. 39) North Centre and Detached Bastion

survive. An arched opening in the brick facade of the former Military Hospital postern (originally with a gate and drawbridge) leads to a tunnel connecting to St. Martin's Battery.

North Centre and Detached Bastion

Begun in 1804, but not finished until 1858-67, the North Centre and Detached Bastion comprises numerous casemated musketry galleries and gun rooms, but also a semi-circular vaulted well passage cut horizontally into the chalk for some 52 feet, ending in a circular chamber. Off the well passage is another shorter passage leading to a second circular well in a square chamber.

South Front Barracks

In the 1860s a great trench was excavated on the side of the hill facing the sea and the bomb-proof South Front Barracks were then built in the trench. Housing 400 men and 91 officers, they were demolished in 1959, but three underground water tanks with a capacity of 100,000 gallons survive. These may have served Archcliffe Fort and the Military Hospital as well as the South Front Barracks.

Western Heights gun batteries: Citadel Battery

There are a number of gun batteries both inside and outside the fortification. By 1900 there were two inside the Citadel, but Citadel Battery was built beyond the Western Outworks between 1898 and 1900 to complement the Langdon Cliff Battery. Together they defended the harbour within a 10 mile radius. Modified for use in the Second World War, the remains,

(Pic. 40) Citadel Battery: gunpit remains

(Pic. 41) Acess to Citadel Battery

reached by steps from a covered way, are underground magazines, store rooms, latrines, ablutions, shelters and a telephone room.

Farthingloe Anti-aircraft Battery

Constructed early in the Second World War west of Citadel Battery, it comprised four gun positions with associated magazines, a control room, shell stores and other buildings. If anything was ever constructed underground, nothing survives.

St. Martin's Battery

St. Martin's Battery was originally built in 1876 near the cliff edge, overlooking the present Western Docks. A main magazine for powder was built underground in 1877 on the other side of South Military Road and was reached through a tunnel from Archcliffe Gate. In the 1890s a new underground cartridge store was provided

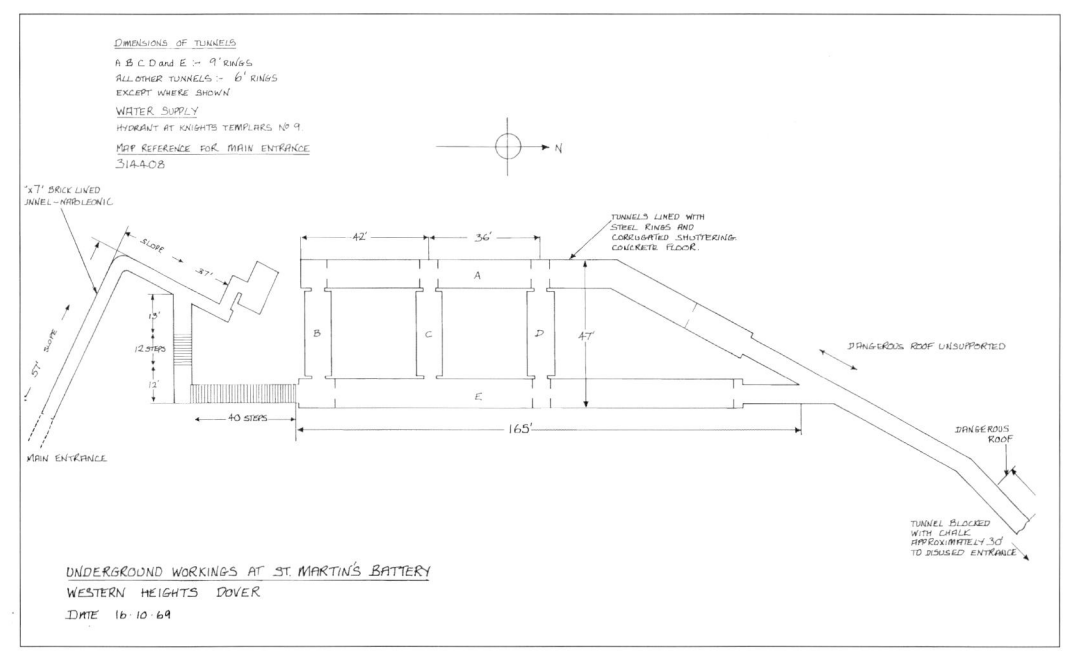

(Pic. 42) St Martin's Battery underground works

(Pic. 43) St Martin's Battery deep shelter

behind the battery via a passage behind the artillery store. The battery was obsolete by the early 1900s, but in 1940 became part of a defensive chain around the coast and named Western Heights Emergency Battery. To accommodate the 150 complement, a larger, deeper shelter with 30 feet (9m) of chalk cover was excavated in the hillside reached by an extension of the tunnel leading to the 1890 cartridge store. Exploration by John Walton and a colleague revealed a Victorian brick-lined sloping tunnel of 94 feet (28m) and 52 steps to the main underground works 165 feet (50m) by 47 feet (14m), comprising two parallel tunnels linked by three shorter tunnels, which were lined with steel rings and corrugated shuttering. Another long tunnel led to a disused entrance, which originally gave onto Grand Shaft Barracks.

South Front Battery

Only one casemate is left of the South Front Battery, but a tunnel survives used for drainage from the Citadel.

(Pic. 44) South Front Battery casemate

(Pic. 45) South Front Battery tunnel

Drop Battery
Built in the 1850s, Drop Battery was in front of the Redoubt on the seaward side armed with eight 8 inch guns. Superseded by the new St. Martin's Battery, it was disarmed in 1886 and by 1925 the site was a small rifle range. The entrances to the underground chambers and passages are now buried, but access to the magazine is possible.

Engineers' Tunnel
Hardly worth a mention is the short tunnel through the ramparts of the Drop Redoubt into the moat which is used today by the public to access the Drop Redoubt on Open Days. It is thought to have been excavated by REs during the Second World War, hence the name.

Pillboxes
Whilst not underground, but to complete the picture of the Heights, early in the Second World War the Heights were circled by pillboxes of which 12 survive. These were some of the 18,000 constructed in Britain during 1940.

Chapter 3
Other underground military installations

In addition to Dover Castle and the Western Heights, there are many other underground works constructed for military purposes mainly during the Second World War.

Fort Burgoyne

Fort Burgoyne is a polygonal fort surrounded by a 35 feet (10.5m) wide ditch and at its centre is a parade ground with bomb proof barracks on three sides. Building began in 1861 and was completed in 1868 to protect the vulnerable north aspect of the castle; its defences were markedly different from those of the Western Heights. There were bomb proof casemates for 130 men and caponiers each with a protected entrance reached via a drawbridge and a vaulted door. Three tunnels gave access from the parade ground to the caponiers. The outworks are located across the Dover/Deal Road and a tunnel under the road links the outworks to the fort. Another tunnel runs from the outworks magazine to a defensive emplacement in its ditch.

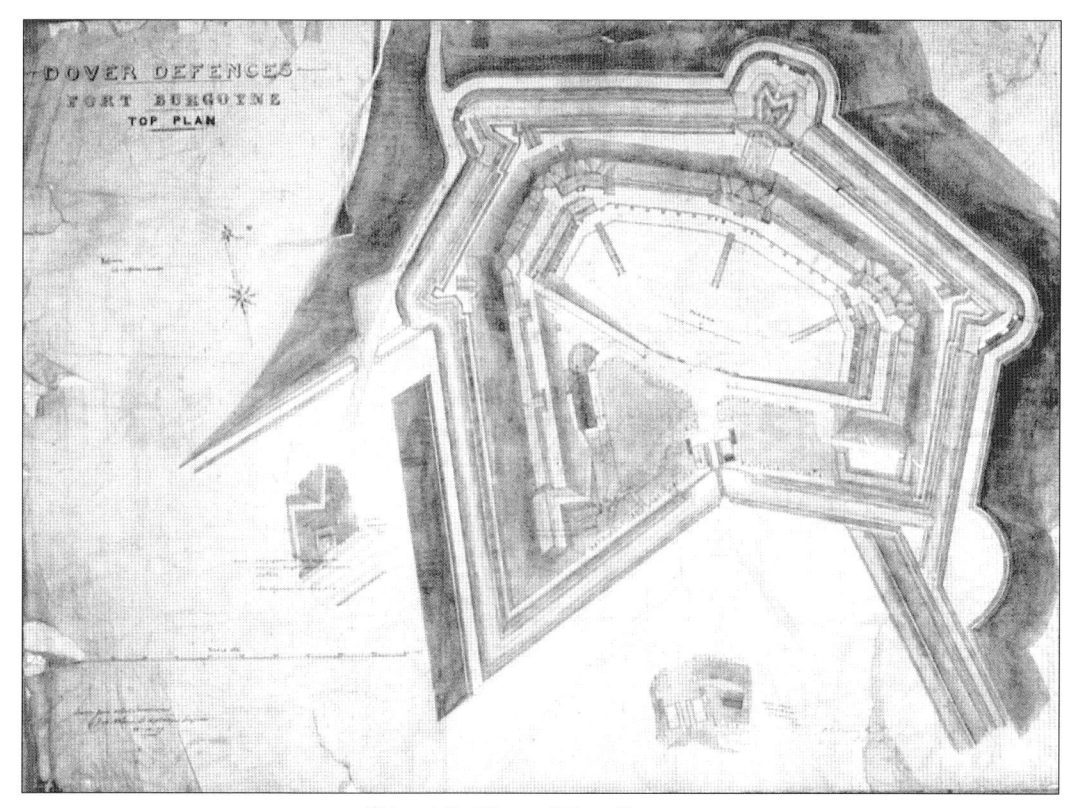

(Pic. 46) Plan of Fort Burgoyne

(Pic. 47) Fort Burgoyne

(Pic. 48) Tunnel from Fort Burgoyne parade ground

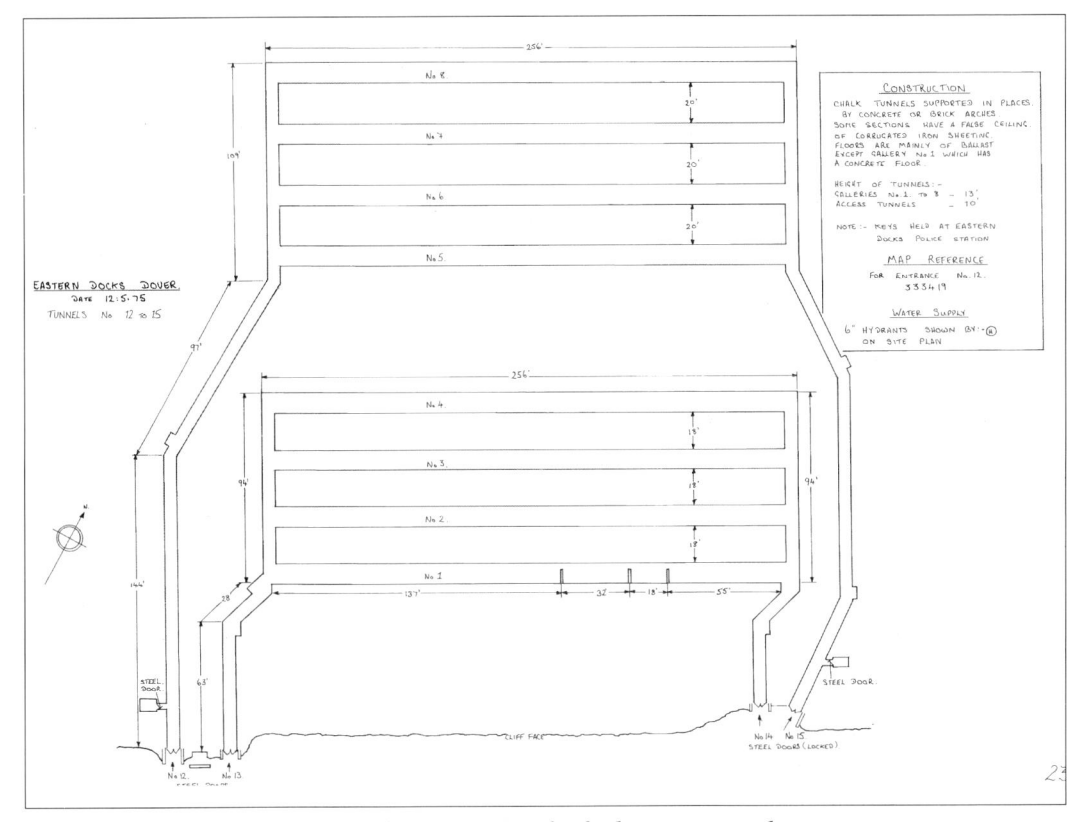

(Pic. 49) Eastern Docks fuel reservoirs plan

Eastern Docks caves

Little known, but perhaps just as amazing as Dover Castle's wartime tunnels, are those excavated during the Second World War in the cliff at ground level in the Eastern Docks where 32 entrances, some now blocked, give access to various cave and tunnel complexes. With war threatening in 1939 the navy began to construct these storage caves for ammunition, mines, torpedoes and fuel. The access tunnels, passageways, and storage caverns were dug, despite the shelling and bombing, 24 hours a day with hand-held compressor tools until they were completed in 1944.

Closest to the dock entrance are 11 entrances to mainly unsupported chalk caves or tunnels. Some are relatively short caves used for storage; others are longer, penetrating up to 80 feet (24m), whilst a series of five, penetrating up to 60 feet (18m), are interconnected.

Beyond the first 11 entrances are another two giving on to tunnels which, after 237 feet, (71m) reach four galleries at right angles to the access tunnels. Another two entrances penetrating 90 feet (27m), lead to another four similar galleries These galleries are 13 feet (13m) high 256 feet (77m) long and vary in width from 18 to 25 feet (5.5 to7.5m). Apparently these were used to store mines. A report in the Dover Express in 1999 told how Les Holyer, aged 39, from Whitfield and employed by Dover Harbour Board was given permission to investigate the Eastern Docks tunnels. He reported that in these caves there were galleries to store mines and ammunition with railway tracks laid on shingle to move them with six sets of tracks side by side to cater for different sized mines. A small train hauled mines to the cave

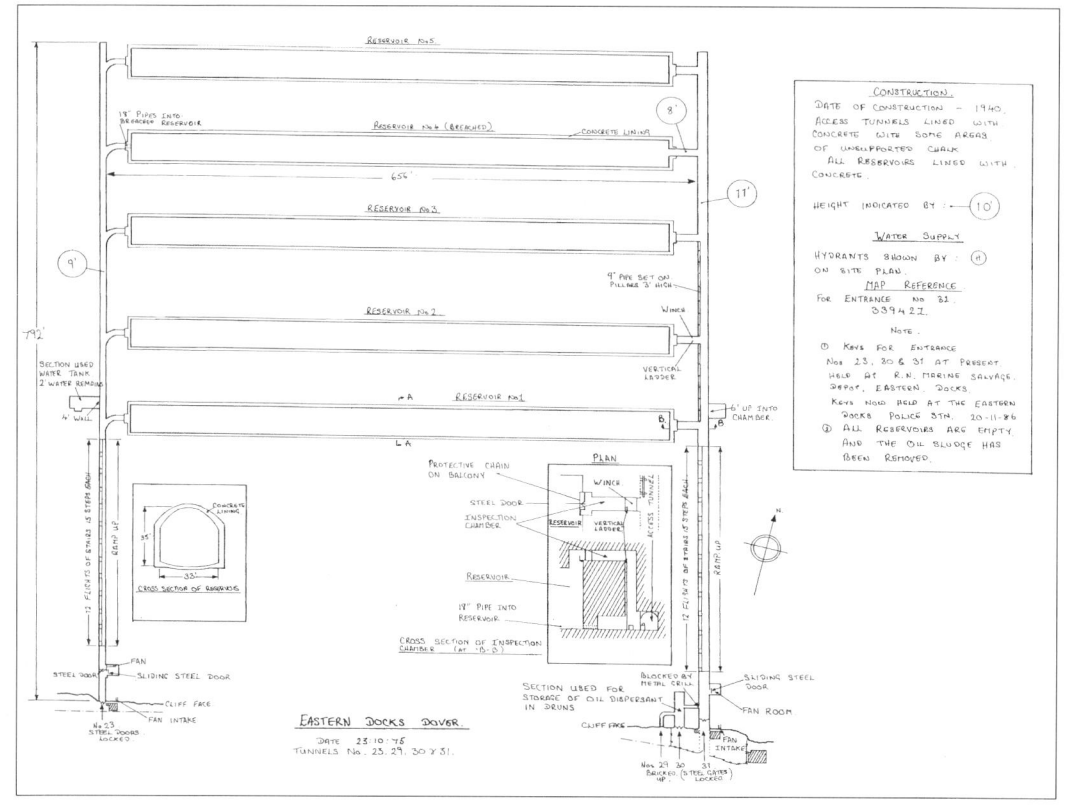

(Pic. 50) Eastern Docks fuel reservoirs plan

entrances where they were unloaded by steam crane and pushed into the caves. Les Holyer also found one small, insignificant cave where coal was kept to fuel the steam cranes. Apparently the steam cranes' boiler lit up the night sky.

The next set of entrances lead to eight petrol storage tanks to fuel Motor Torpedo Boats and air/sea rescue launches operating out of Dover Harbour. The three parallel 12 feet (3.5m) square storage tunnels of unsupported chalk are 18 feet (5.5m) above ground level and penetrate 165 feet (50m) with two 3 feet (1m) wide and 7 feet (2m) high access tunnels between them half the length, which ended at a communicating tunnel 146 feet (44m) at right angles to the storage tunnels. Once the metal storage tanks, each being 30 feet (9m) by 90 feet (28m) with a capacity of 12,000 gallons (54,000 litres), had been pushed through their tunnels into position, their entrances were sealed, leaving room only for personnel and the necessary pipelines.

There is another much smaller complex with five entrances that 'meanders' more or less parallel with the cliff face. Yet another entrance sits above, leading to a short tunnel running parallel with the cliff face and a short spur further into the cliff. The next two entrances lead to relatively small caves.

Further to the east, enormous underground fuel reservoirs were excavated with the aim of providing enough fuel to supply the Home Fleet for ten days. During construction sand, ballast and cement were carried on a conveyor belt to a safe working area which also removed chalk waste to be dumped in Langdon Bay. Work carried on around the clock using only pneumatic drills and pickaxes; as the miners finished, concreters and carpenters moved in. Two entrances were made with access tunnels about 1000 feet (300m) long, one 6 feet (2m) wide and 8 feet (2.5m) high and the other 10 feet (3m) wide and 8 feet (2.5m) high. There was a fan house with a fan to extract or draw in air from cliff face. One tunnel had 11 flights of stairs each 15 steps (165 in all) and the other 12 flights of 15 steps making 180 in total. At the top of the stairs was a ladder 40 feet (12m) long to a platform, followed by a similar ladder to the five 3 feet (1m) thick concrete-lined oil tanks, cathedral-like with arched ceilings, each 32 feet (10m) wide, 40 feet (12m) deep by 600 feet (180m) long with a total capacity of 18,500 tons or 4,155,741 gallons (18,892,000 litres). Only one tank contained diesel, the remainder furnace oil. A simple float in the oil connected to an external gauge indicated the contents at all times. An 800 feet (240m) long tunnel with 18 inch (45cm) pipes connected the reservoirs to the Eastern Arm to receive the oil from tankers and to supply RN vessels.

Furthest away from the docks entrance is an access leading after 36 feet (11m) to a small complex of tunnels but with a diagonal tunnel staircase going up 643 feet (198m) to an entrance/exit in front of the present Saga National Trust building on Langdon Cliffs. This interesting feature is now used to house a water main to the Eastern Docks. Dating from about 1897, the original purpose of the staircase is thought to have been for prisoners in Langdon Prison at the top of the cliff to work on the construction of the National Harbour; however, there was an outcry, apparently, from local people fearing that prisoners would escape as well as depriving them of jobs and so it was not used.

The Les Holyer newspaper report stated that some caves had running water, flush toilets and air conditioning. There were offices, an RN accident department for treatment, including minor operations, as well as a mortuary. All the caves were used by the Navy except one for Royal Marine engineers who built the submarine pens.

This complex was finished in 1944 and was used before the end of the war but not emptied of fuel until 1968. In 1991 the Ministry of Defence handed it all over to the Dover Harbour Board. Various suggestions for its use have been made, including wine storage, mushroom farming, sand and ballast storage and even a multi-storey car park. Perhaps it is best left as a reminder to future generations of the lengths Britain was prepared to go in order to defend the country. Unfortunately, situated in the high security area of the Eastern Docks and being so hazardous, there is no prospect of it being opened to the public.

Gun batteries and associated works

During the Second World War many gun batteries and associated works were constructed in the Dover area to protect the coast and to intercept enemy aircraft. Many had underground compartments. With the installation of long range guns came underground control posts with accommodation for the crews. Batteries to the east and west of Dover were each designated as a fortress and each fortress had an underground plotting room (FPR) from where their guns were controlled. Each separate gun battery within the fortress had a similar underground plotting room (BPR) controlling its own guns. These rooms were equipped with table-top maps of the Strait on which targets were plotted. Information came from the battery observation posts on the cliff edge. Later radar was used. Other underground works were used as deep shelters for gun crews and first aid posts.

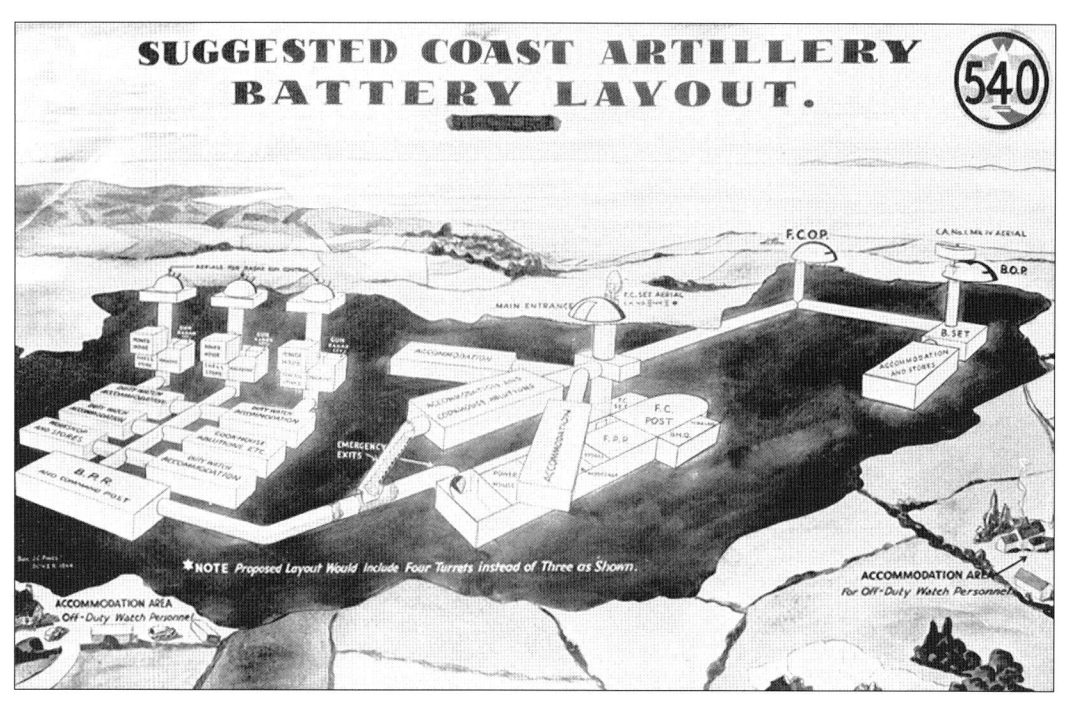

(Pic. 51) Suggested coastal artillery battery layout (SECRET blacked out)

(Pic. 52) Coastal battery gun

Capel Battery

When travelling eastward from Folkestone, Capel Battery is the first of the Dover coastal batteries. Built between 1941 and 1942, it was located on the present Battle of Britain Memorial site. The site proved difficult for tunnelling since amongst the chalk was clay and sand. In April 1941 this caused a serious collapse whilst tunnelling was in progress and three REs were buried, two of whom died. The guns for both this and Hougham Battery were supplied, on Winston Churchill's orders, by removing guns from the cruisers HMS *Norfolk*, *Dorsetshire* and *York*. The buildings above ground were demolished in 1980, but surviving underground and reached by 123 steps, are a deep shelter, dressing station, battery plotting room and magazines albeit in a poor state, buried and sealed.

(Pics. 53, 54) Capel Battery: Underground construction

(Pic. 55) Capel Battery gun

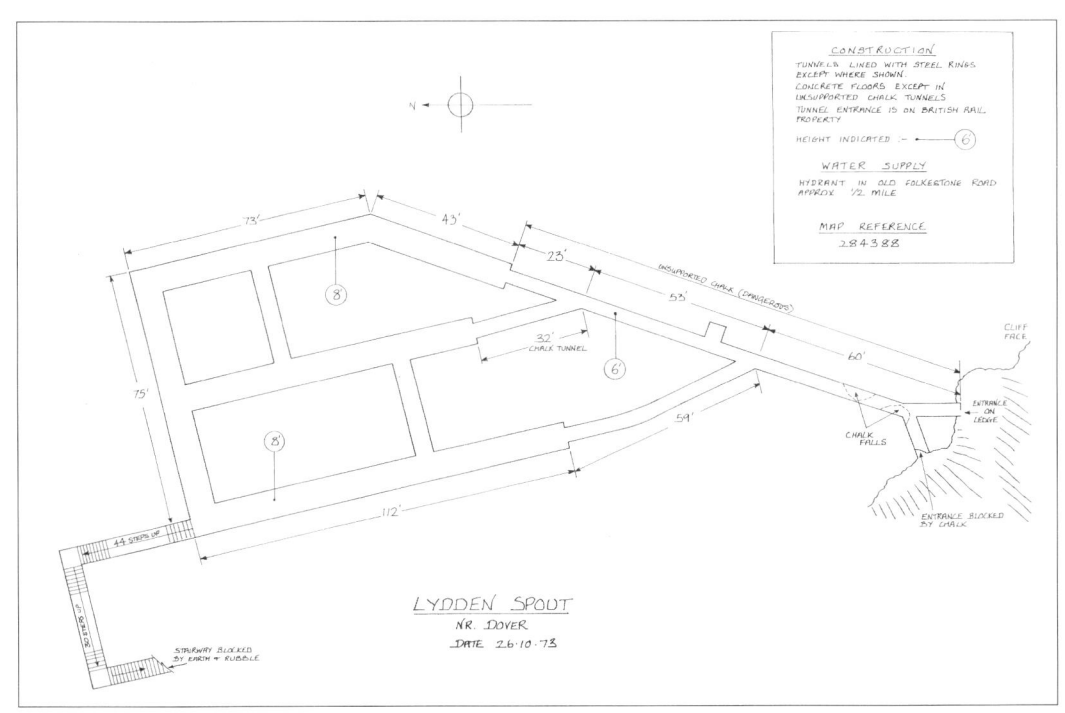

(Pic. 56) Lydden Spout deep shelter plan

(Pic. 57) Lydden Spout deep shelter

(Pic. 58) Lydden Spout deep shelter

(Pic. 59) Hougham Battery plotting room under construction

Lydden Spout Battery

Lydden Spout Battery was constructed in 1941. Although the three gun positions were demolished in the 1970s as eyesores, some surface buildings survive. Below ground are a plotting room, magazines and a deep shelter reached from the cliff face via a tunnel 136 feet (41m) long. The complex is partly lined with steel rings and partly unsupported chalk. An alternative entrance begins with 74 steps up.

Hougham Battery

Hougham Battery, built in 1941, was equipped with three 8 inch guns and included nine underground rooms of similar design to Capel Battery. It was located on the cliffs in the side of a small chalk quarry above what is now Samphire Hoe with observation posts on the cliff edge. Entrance to the underground section was via an inclined ramp on the cliffs or via a tunnel from the accommodation further inland. All the surface buildings of the battery were demolished to make way for the A20 road into Dover. Surviving underground, however, are a combined fortress and battery plotting room plus three magazines for the guns.

Situated behind the Hougham Battery gun sites was a separate dressing station, which survives. A tunnel from the main entrance reaches a fork after 272 feet (82m) with the choice of steps leading to a blocked tunnel or a 297 feet (89m) long tunnel leading to yet another tunnel with a chute alongside 120 steps. At the end was a winch arrangement and an alternative entrance. Built in 1942, construction was typical of the time with steel rings and corrugated shuttering. The complex was used for fire safety training in the 1980s by Channel Tunnel workers.

Lydden Bunkers

Moving away from the coast, on Lydden Hill there was an ammunition dump housed in three large buildings plus a tunnel used as an air raid shelter, but it no longer exists.

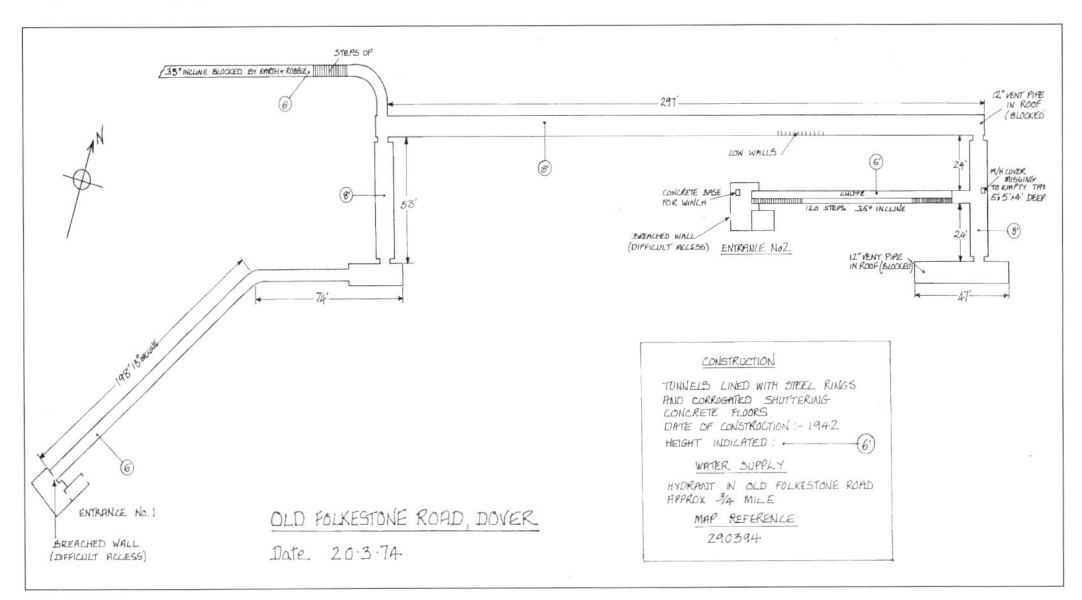

(Pic. 60) Hougham dressing station plan

Drellingore Platoon

With the threat of a German invasion during the Second World War small specialist platoons of six men from the Home Guard, nicknamed scallywags, were formed whose task would have been to carry out sabotage attacks behind enemy lines. Each platoon was independent and based in a secret, underground bunker. The bunker for the Drellingore Platoon was carved out of the hillside in the Alkham Valley. Only the concrete entrance shaft survives but it would have contained bunk beds, a stove, lamp, water tank, food and sabotage equipment.

North Military Road

Closer to the coast on the steep hill of North Military Road is a solid concrete building used currently as a car repair workshop, but during the Second World War it was apparently an ammunition store. Inside there is a vertical shaft in the floor, which the owner heard was used to lower or lift ammunition onto or off trucks on the railway line in the tunnel at the bottom of the shaft. It is more likely that it was built by the Royal Electrical and Mechanical Engineers to service the long range guns.

Langdon Prison/Barracks site (now the National Trust/Saga site)

Back on the coast at the Langdon Cliffs National Trust Saga site a small underground U-shaped shelter survives from the Second World War. Two entrances provide access to 20 feet (6m) long tunnels into the cliff before 90° turns connect them to each other after 36 feet (11m). From this site there is also a much older tunnel and stairway giving access to the rear of the Eastern Arm (see Eastern Docks above).

Langdon Lights

Langdon Lights were three searchlight batteries that could be reached from the cliff top at Langdon Bay by a steep zig-zag path, known as Langdon Stairs, or from the base of the cliffs via a retractable ladder. They were built into the cliff face to illuminate passing ships for identification. Graffiti on the chalk walls indicate occupation during the First World War. Only two sites remain due to cliff falls.

At the top of the stairs, above ground, was a generator room. From it a

(Pic. 61) Langdon lights

(Pic. 62) Langdon lights

(Pic. 63) Langdon Battery tunnel

24 feet (7m) long chalk tunnel only 3 feet wide (1m) and high leads to an underground chamber 12 feet (3.6m) by 6 feet (2m), which was presumably an air raid shelter.

Langdon Battery

Built around 1900 to protect the new Admiralty Harbour, Langdon Battery was used in both wars and was originally equipped with three 9 inch guns and later two 6 inch guns. The Dover Coastguard building now covers the site, but some underground sections below the former gun positions survive and are now used for storage and a staff gym, but the magazines are sealed. A tunnel links the

(Pic. 64) Langdon Hole deep shelter

Langdon Hole Deep Shelter

Behind Langdon Battery Langdon Hole Deep Shelter survives, comprising two long parallel tunnels of 89 feet (27m) connected at both ends by 43 feet (13m) long tunnels. The tunnels are lined with steel shuttering and iron girders give support. One entrance involves 80 steps over 150 feet (45m) and a second has 105 steps over 120 feet (36m). Both Langdon Hole and Long Hill (see below) were probably communications satellites of Dover Castle, often called Dumpy A (Long Hill) and Dumpy B (Langdon Hole) and are of similar construction.

site with the former observation post on the cliff edge.

(Pic. 65) Langdon Hole deep shelter

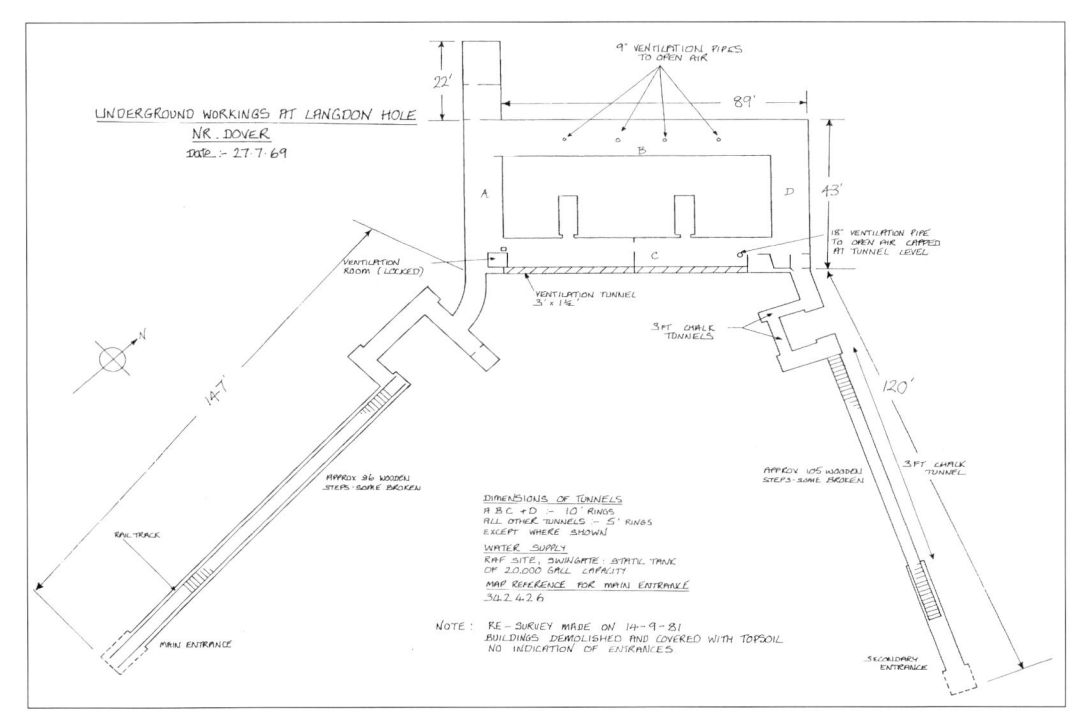

(Pic. 66) Plan of Langdon Hole

(Pic. 67) Long Hill / Roman Road deep shelter

Long Hill/ Roman Road Deep Shelter

Inland the Long Hill Deep Shelter off Roman Road was apparently built as a radio station for the RAF in 1937 and is very similar to Langdon Hole Deep Shelter. A 273 feet (82m) entrance tunnel leads to a rectangle of tunnels with another tunnel of 170 feet (51m) leading to a second entrance.

Swingate Chain Home Station

Following the British invention of radar in the 1930s four transmitting towers 350 feet (105m) high and four receiving towers were erected at Swingate. These formed part of a chain of 47 similar sites, which proved vital in the Battle of Britain by giving warning of approaching enemy aircraft. After the war the US Air Force used them for communications in southern England and they are now used for television transmission, although only two towers, only one of which is original, survive. As part of the Cold War precautions a Royal Observer Corps post was built in 1962 which closed in 1968. During the period 1960-68 870 similar posts were constructed in Britain. From the surface a vertical shaft and ladder led to a complex 25 feet (7.5m) below, comprising one main work room plus accommodation and toilets. Built of reinforced concrete, these posts were nuclear blast and radiation proof.

(Pic. 68) Swingate Chain Home Station aerials

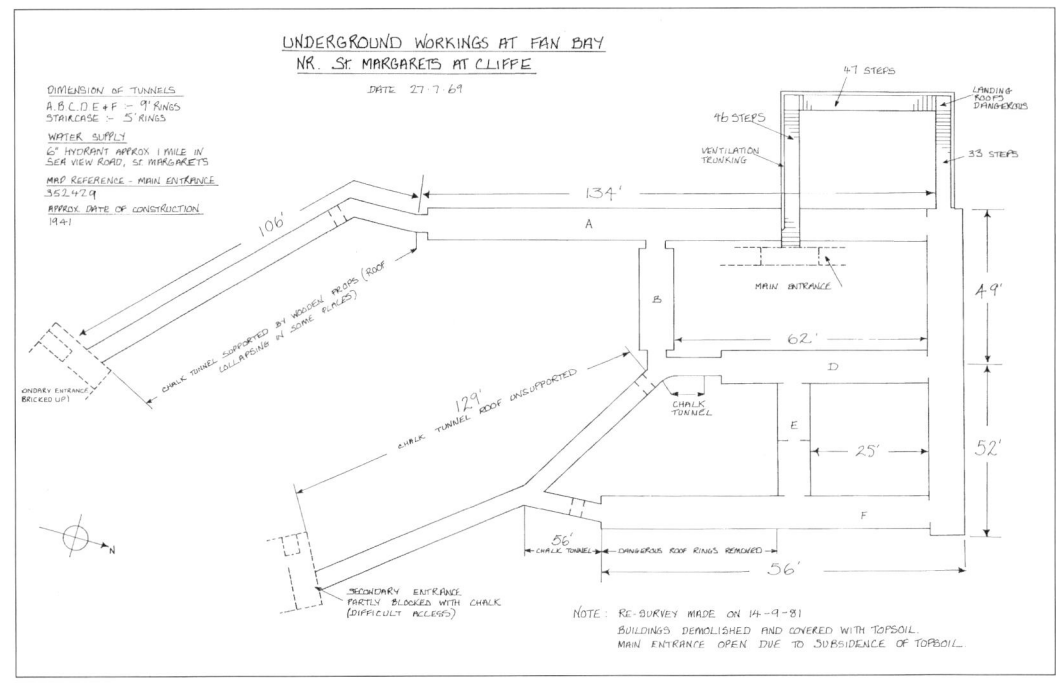

(Pic. 69) Fan Bay Deep Shelter plan

Fan Bay Battery

Fan Bay Battery was located on the cliffs above the dip in the landscape known as Fan Hole and was excavated in 1941 by 172 Tunnelling Company REs who left behind a great deal of graffiti in the chalk. Similar to Lydden Spout Battery, it had three 6 inch guns with a deep shelter that could house 189 men, plotting room, magazines and accommodation. All the surface buildings were demolished as eyesores in the 1970s, but the underground magazines and the deep shelter remain. Construction of the shelter, which is the largest and best-preserved deep shelter in the Dover area, is typical of the

(Pic. 70) Fan Bay Deep Shelter

(Pics.71, 72) Fan Bay Deep Shelter

time with steel shuttering and iron girders. From the main entrance 126 steps lead to the complex which extends up to 134 feet (40m) in one direction and 100 feet (30m) in the other. Two unsupported chalk tunnels each over 100 feet (30m) long lead to secondary entrances. Separate from and closer to the cliff face than the FPR was a typical BPR layout accessed by two vertical shafts with ladders.

Wanstone Farm Battery

Wanstone Farm Battery, constructed in 1941, was the largest of Dover's coastal batteries with two 15 inch guns called Jane and Clem (named after the Daily Mirror's saucy cartoon character, Jane and Churchill's wife, Clementine) each with 2 magazines. The complex included a sergeants' mess in the farmhouse, officers' mess, NAAFI, guardroom, workshops, power rooms, observation posts, underground plotting rooms and a deep shelter. Used for training by the Coastal Training Regiment until the 1950s, many of the surface buildings have since been demolished, but the underground works survive in good condition on private land. The 103 feet (31m) long main entrance tunnel to the underground shelter gives onto two parallel tunnels 10 to 12 feet (3 to 3.6m) wide each over 200 feet (60m) long and connected by three tunnels 28 feet (8.4m) long. An alternative entrance tunnel is 110 feet (33m) in length. The battery plotting room still exists. Local historian, David Collyer, was told that at Wanstone Farm there was also a hide for the local section of Home Guard Auxiliary Units. These secret volunteer units would have undertaken sabotage behind enemy lines if Britain was invaded.

(Pic. 73) Wanstone Farm 15 inch gun

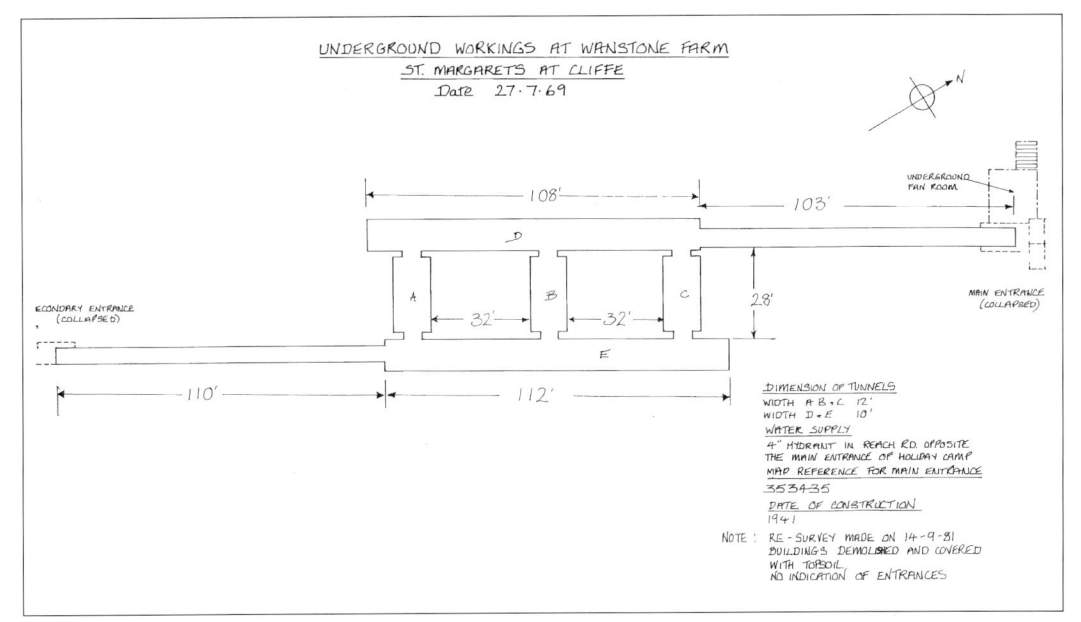

(Pic. 74) Wanstone Farm Battery plan

(Pic. 75) Wanstone Farm Battery under construction

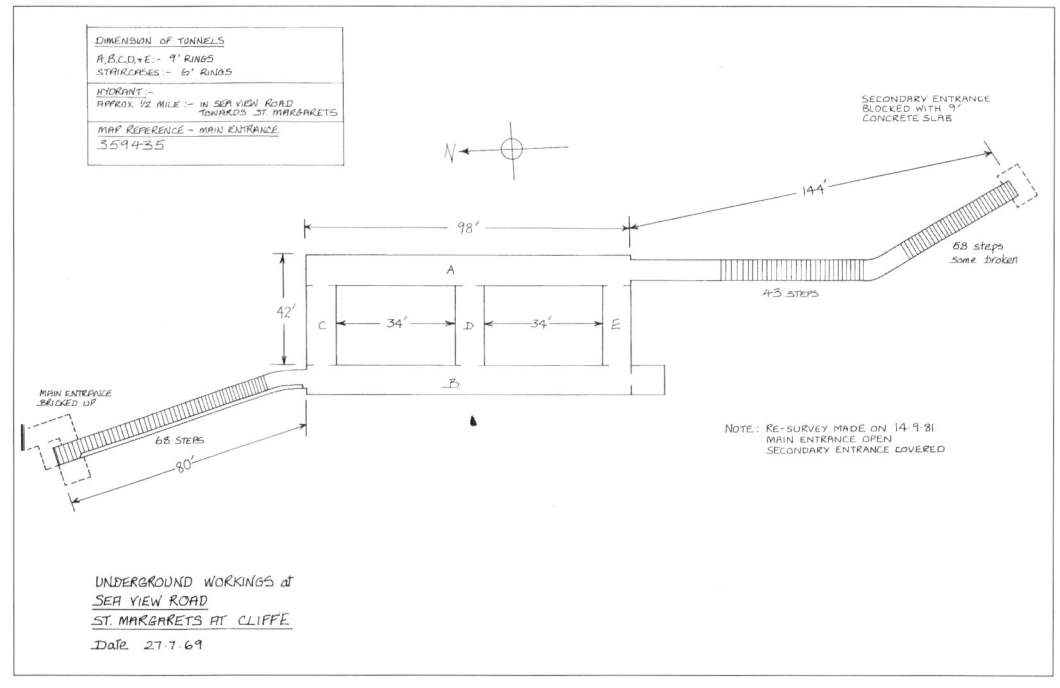

(Pic. 76) South Foreland Battery plan Seaview Road

South Foreland Battery

Dating from 1940, South Foreland Battery with four guns occupied a large site at the end of Lighthouse Road, St. Margaret's. Most of the surface buildings have gone, but the underground works survive, including the battery and fortress plotting rooms. The fortress plotting room shared a tunnelled shelter with the Regimental Headquarters of 540 Coastal Defence Regiment which was alongside the South Foreland lighthouse. The complex is reached by two sets of stairways, 68 steps covering 80 feet (24m) and 100 steps over 144 feet (43m), either end of the two 100 feet (30m) long tunnels which are interconnected by three 36 feet (11m) long tunnels. To the rear of the site of gun position 2 is the vast battery shelter with three stairways, two of them 100 feet (30m) long and the other 75 feet (22.5m), leading into two parallel tunnels 150 feet (45m) long connected by three 50 feet (15m) long

(Pic. 77) South Foreland plotting room 2

tunnels housing medical services and sleeping accommodation. All are lined with steel rings with corrugated shuttering and concrete floors. The main tunnels were also lined with plywood and tarred paper.

Townsend Farm Dressing Station

This dressing station served the two gun sites housing 'Winnie' west of St. Margaret's and 'Pooh' east of St Margaret's. Six different entrances with steps down lead to a main tunnel 276 feet (83m) long connected to a parallel tunnel. Construction is mainly unsupported chalk.

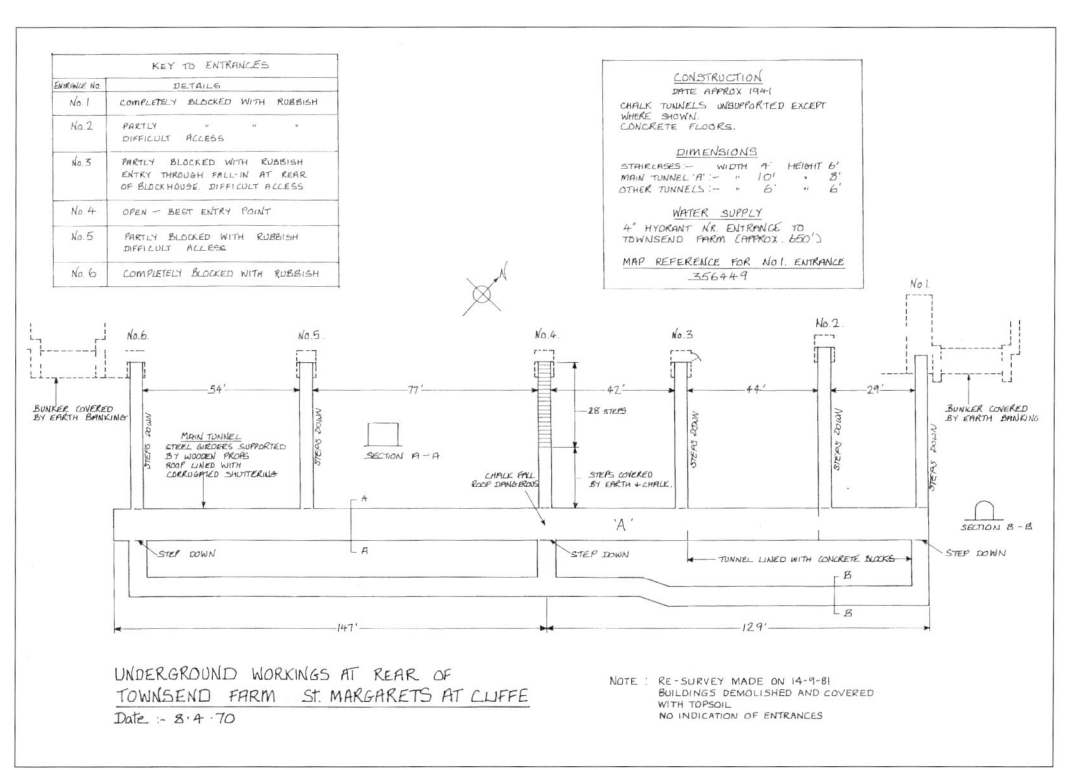

(Pic. 78) South Foreland deep shelter

(Pic. 79) Townsend Farm Dressing Station plan

(Pic. 80) St Margaret's Bay Esplanade Tunnel

(Pic. 81) St Margaret's Bay Esplanade Tunnel

Esplanade Tunnel, St Margaret's Bay

A sealed entrance in the cliff at the western end of the Esplanade at St. Margaret's Bay conceals a 300 feet (90m) long tunnel 6 feet 6 (2m) high, mainly brick-lined with a galvanized corrugated iron roof, which led to two separate machine gun posts cut into the cliff face, one of which is still visible some 20 feet (6m) above beach level. A flight of rough stairs cut into the chalk led to the second machine gun post, which with erosion now resembles a balcony overlooking the sea.

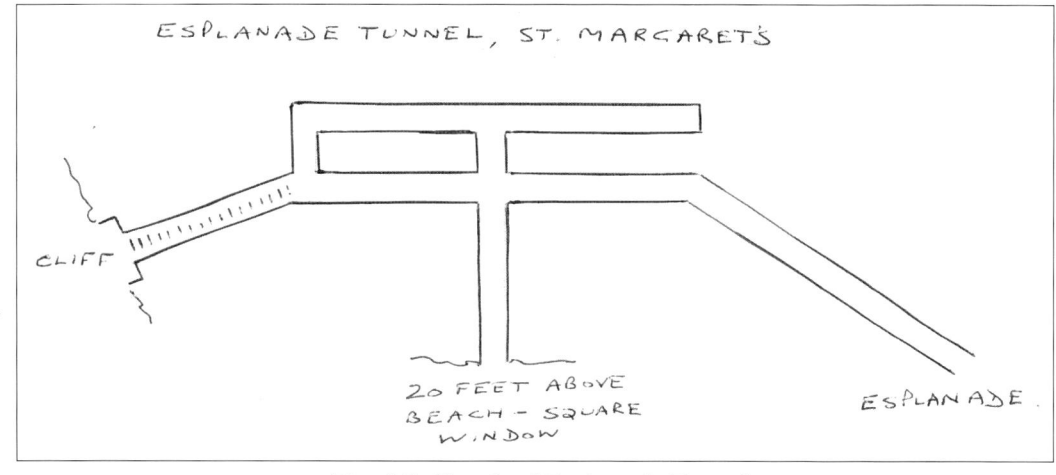

(Pic. 82) Sketch of Esplanade Tunnel

St. Margaret's Battery

Situated on the cliff edge above St. Margaret's Bay, the battery's guns came from HMS *Hood*. Behind the four gun positions, demolished in the 1970s, reached by a long tunnel was a deep shelter situated behind Granville Road, providing 60 feet (18m) of cover, to accommodate the 169 personnel plus medical services. It consists of the usual two parallel tunnels some 200 feet (60m) long connected by narrower tunnels with another two entrances.

RAF site The Droveway, St. Margaret's

The RAF site at The Droveway, St Margaret's was built in the 1950s behind the Dover Patrol Memorial to accommodate a top secret radar station able to give early warning of a nuclear attack. It was closed in 1960 but maintained until 1982 when all the surface buildings were demolished except for the guardroom which is now a private bungalow. The guard room

(Pic. 83) Access tunnel to St Margaret's Battery underground works

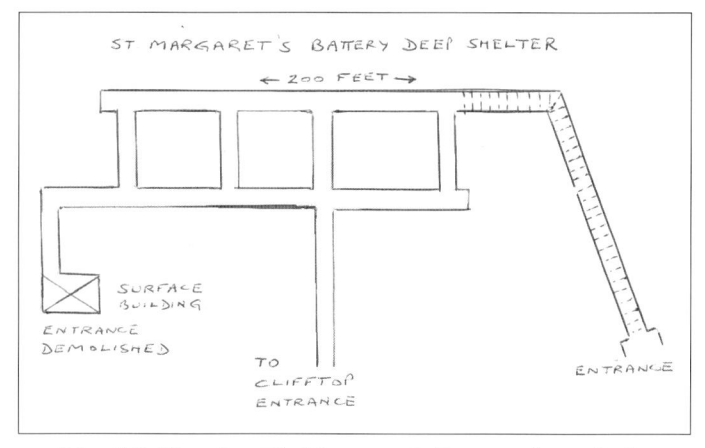

(Pic. 84) Sketch of St Margaret's Battery deep shelter

concealed an access corridor to a deep bunker containing protected operational rooms. From the former guardroom a 325 feet (98m) long entrance tunnel leads to the main complex encased in reinforced concrete with six rooms lined with cork insulation off a main corridor, an air conditioning plant and an emergency exit at the far end.

According to David Collyer, the pile of excavated chalk was as high as the memorial during construction. When the new station was commissioned, it is said that a telegram was received from the Russian Embassy congratulating the Ministry of Defence! Another story

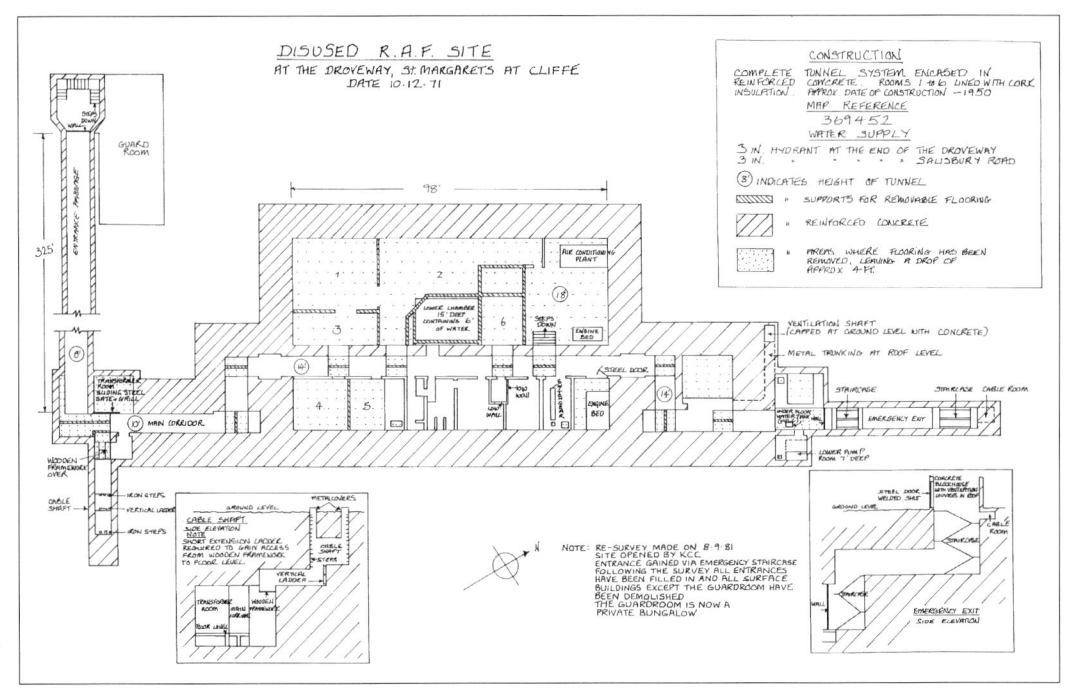

(Pic. 85) RAF site The Droveway plan

is that RAF guards were apparently mystified how courting couples kept finding their way within the barbed wire perimeter until they discovered an exit from the old St. Margaret's Battery magazines.

Bluebird Tea Rooms, Leathercote Point

On the cliff top by the Dover Patrol Memorial a coastguard lookout, built in 1932, is now in use as tea rooms with fantastic views over the Channel. Some 40 feet (12m) below the building, reached originally by two separate wooden staircases and a short passage, is an air raid shelter with corrugated iron roof, dating from 1940 when the building is thought to have been an observation post.

PART TWO
CIVILIAN CAVES AND TUNNELS

Chapter 1
Civilian descriptions

In addition to underground works for military purposes the Dover area is riddled with caves and tunnels excavated for civilian purposes, including storage, industry, transport and shelter from aerial bombardment during the two world wars. These are described below taking them in a west to east order, although the list may not be exhaustive since there are many small, private caves not mentioned as well as rumours of others not traced.

Channel tunnels

Whilst I have excluded railway tunnels from my research, mention must be made of the Channel Tunnel. Plans for a Channel tunnel by Albert Mathieu, complete with ventilation

(Pic. 86) 1880 Channel Tunnel

(Pic. 87) 1990 Channel Tunnel break through

shafts cum chimneys towering above the sea and designed for horse and carriage to drive through, appeared as early as 1802. At the same time de Mottray, another French engineer, planned a submerged, watertight tube to rest on the sea bed with unevenness remedied by cuttings and embankments. Later, Aimé Thomé de Gamond had various ideas for a fixed link, including a viaduct of granite and steel, a floating island and a man-made causeway with swing bridges for passing ships. He became convinced, however, that a bored tunnel would be the most practical and in 1856 proposed a circular, stone tunnel with two railway tracks. A man-made island on the Varne Bank, which is only 15 feet (4.5m) below the surface, would be an international station! This scheme was stopped in its tracks with Britain's fear of Napoleon III.

In the 1850s a British mining engineer, William Low, designed twin tunnels each with a single railway track, connected at intervals by cross-tunnels – very similar to the tunnel eventually built almost 150 years later! The Channel Tunnel Company was formed in 1872 to carry out the scheme at an estimated cost of £10 million. Test-boring was carried out in St. Margaret's Bay and, with both countries having authorised a tunnel in 1875, preliminary trials began, but work was abandoned in 1877 due to flooding. Having established that an unbroken stretch of suitable chalk, impervious, relatively soft and up to 170 feet (51m) thick, spanned the Channel, another tunnel was started by Sir Edward Watkin MP, Chairman of the South East Railway, at Shakespeare Cliff in 1880. A 74 feet (22.5m) shaft was sunk next to the SER line at Abbots Cliff and a 7 feet (2m) diameter pilot tunnel was cut by one of the first tunnelling machines, whilst from the French end traditional methods of pick and shovel were used. A second shaft was sunk 160 feet (48m) down with another pilot tunnel which, it was hoped, would meet the French tunnellers in the middle of the Channel. Eventually a double tunnel 14 feet (4m) in diameter would be excavated with cross passages and lined with concrete. Trains were to be drawn through the tunnel by air-compressed locomotives at 30 miles an hour. At the Dover terminus a vast underground station was envisaged where whole trains would be raised to the surface by hydraulic lifts. The Victorians really thought big! Fears of invasion via such a tunnel were countered by Sir Edward stating that, if necessary, as well as being fortified, the tunnel could be disabled by flooding, filling with steam, blocking with shingle or detonating explosives; nevertheless, after excavating 6,000 feet (1800m), the government forced the abandonment of the project in 1882. Today, the remains are used as a drainage tunnel for the Dover to Folkestone railway track.

Sir Edward tried again in 1892 with a new shaft 2,222 feet (666m) deep into a coal seam, which was then mined and the original tunnel workings filled in.

Other schemes for a tunnel were proposed, although sometimes the timing was bad with one just before the outbreak of the Great War in 1914 and another in 1939. Yet another attempt actually started in 1922, using a machine that could excavate a 12 feet (3.5m) diameter circle at 12 feet (3.5m) an hour. After only 400 feet (120m), however, the tunnelling machine broke down and was abandoned! Another proposal in 1930 was rejected. The idea surfaced again in 1942 as a way of supplying allied troops after D-Day, but it was thought the war would be over before a tunnel could be completed!

It was not until 1964 that there was a real prospect of a fixed link between Britain and France when the two governments agreed in principle to its construction. A trial tunnel 820 feet (246m) long was dug in 1973 6,500 feet (2km) under the sea, but once again the scheme was abandoned, this time due to cost, only to be revived again in 1986 with a treaty signed by Prime Minister Margaret Thatcher and President Mitterand. Eleven privately financed schemes were submitted, but the Channel Tunnel Group's (later renamed Eurotunnel) twin-bored tunnel taking shuttle trains and through trains was chosen. Work began in 1987. Over a period of seven years 13,000 workers were employed excavating two main tunnels plus a service tunnel 31 miles (50km) in length. On 30 October 1990 French and British tunnellers met each other in the pilot tunnel under the Channel, making it possible to walk from Britain to France, followed by the service tunnels meeting in December. Tunnelling was completed in 1991 with the British spoil, totalling 5 million cubic yards, forming a new platform of land at the foot of the cliffs, later named Samphire Hoe. The tunnel was opened for use in 1994 at an estimated cost of £10,000 million.

Warren Halt well shaft

On the cliffs between Dover and Folkestone there is a deep vertical shaft lined with sleepers and braced with iron hoops which provides access, with the help of an iron ladder, to a drainage system. At the foot of the shaft is a tunnel now lined with corrugated and galvanized steel, which goes inland underneath the Dover/Folkestone railway line to a dead end. The other direction seawards ends at a locked entrance on the concrete apron of the Warren. A continuous stream of water runs through the tunnel. This is apparently one of about 20 similar drainage tunnels under this stretch of railway line.

South Military Hill

Keith Slade describes three caves at South Military Hill with no known purpose: two of them roughly 20 feet (6m) by 50 feet (15m) and 20 feet (6m) high and the third 100 feet (30m) long. Graffiti on the chalk wall read, 'J. Parrish 1852'. A 2010 visit found four openings in the cliff face covered in by large chalk blocks. They are mentioned in an 1836 Dover guide, but, since there appears to be no connection with the Western Heights fortifications close by, these caves could well have been excavations of chalk for the local lime making business. Another more exciting suggestion is that they were excavated to house guns to guard the entrance to an early Channel Tunnel project that was to start from Hawkesbury Street in the old Pier District, although no evidence of any such project exists.

(Pic. 88) Caves on South Military Hill overlooking the Western Docks

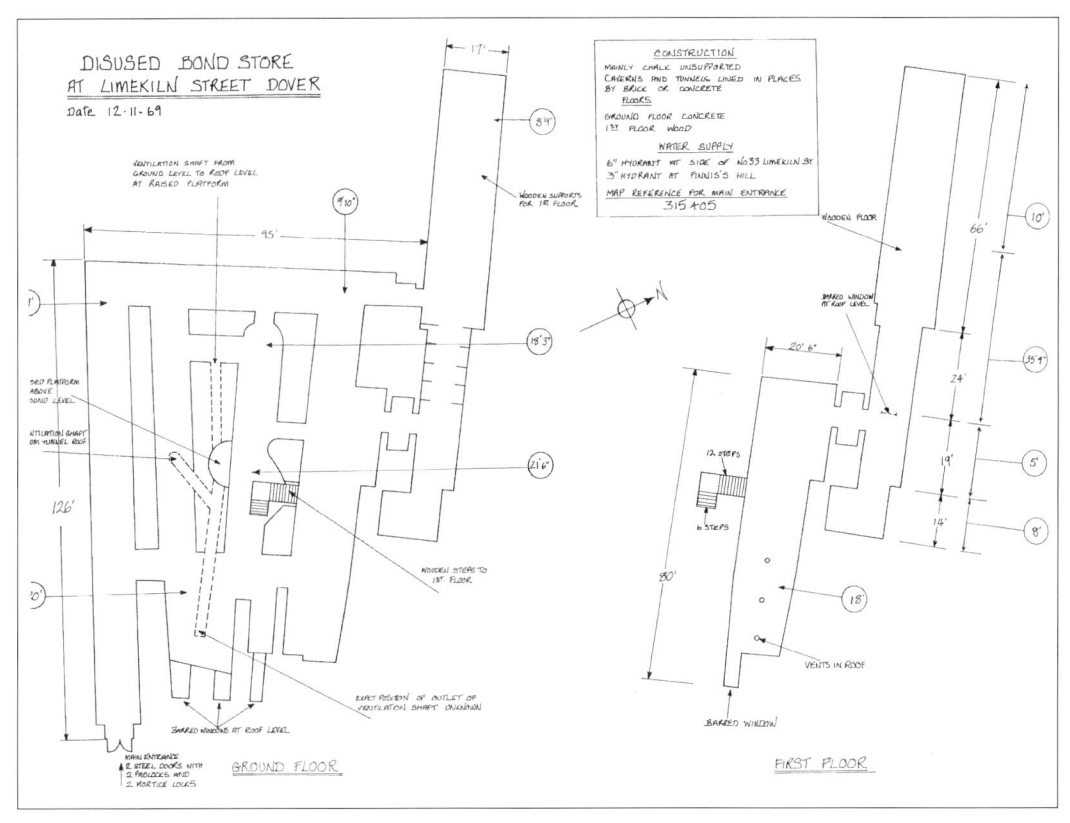

(Pic. 89) Champagne Caves plan

Channel View Road Cave

Opposite the rear of the P&O Building in Channel View Road is a brick-lined cave 50 feet (15m) deep, 10 feet (3m) wide and high. This was probably the air raid shelter for the pupils of Archcliffe Road School (Pier Infants).

Limekiln Street Bonded Store/Champagne Caves

The origin of this large tunnel complex, situated west of the Oil Mill caves, is unknown. It was possibly dug as a source of lime initially and dates back to at least the mid 19th century. It is said to have been used as a bonded warehouse (where imported goods could be stored without paying the high Customs duty until they were removed), hence the reason for two of its names: Bonded Store and Champagne Caves. During the Second World War it was used to shelter several hundred people. The roof is very high in places where once there was an upper floor. These caverns and tunnels are mainly unsupported chalk, lined in places with brick or concrete. The main complex at the lower level comprises four tunnels but with only one entrance penetrating 126 feet (38m) across 95 feet (29m) with a connection to another tunnel 17 feet wide. Unusually there are three windows at roof level at the cliff edge. In 1969 when John Walton mapped these caves 18 steps led to an upper level to a cavern 20 feet (6m) wide and 80 feet (24m) long, which, in turn, led to a cavern 134 feet (940m) long with a wooden floor above one of the lower level caverns. There is no connection with the Upper and Lower Oil Mill Caves to the east.

(Pics.90, 91) Champagne Caves

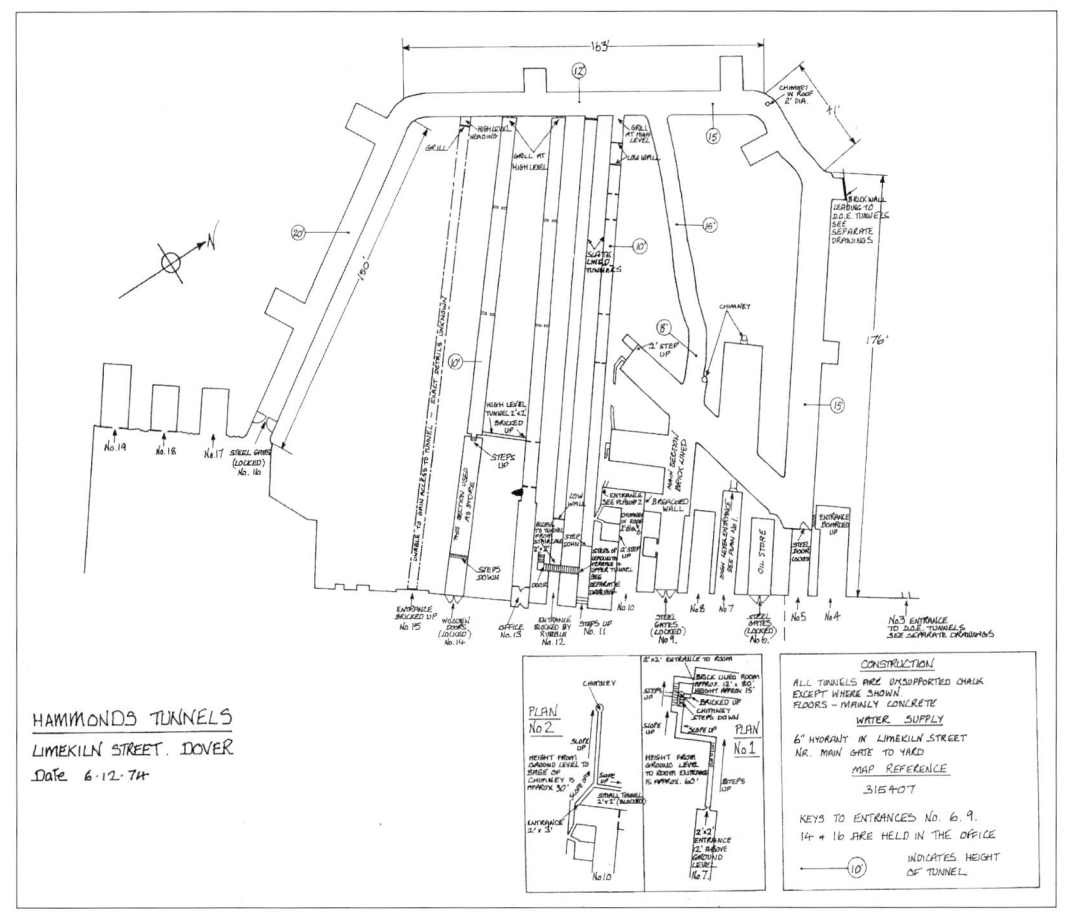

(Pic. 92) Lower Oil Mill Caves plan

Oil Mill/Hammonds Caves

These tunnels in Limekiln Street were also probably dug originally to extract chalk for lime, but have had various uses over the years, particularly storage. Lime kilns nearby gave the street its name. This complex is virtually impossible to describe. There are 19 entrances leading either to short self-contained caves or to the main complex of mainly unsupported chalk. At ground level, known as the Lower Oil Mill Caves, one tunnel covering three sides of a rectangle forms the exterior boundary penetrating 175 feet (53m). Within it are five parallel tunnels at 90° to the cliff face with yet another more complex layout. In places the tunnels are cavernous and 30 feet (9m) high. There is evidence of alteration over the years, particularly when used as air raid shelters during both world wars. The caves were damaged by a huge fire in March 1957, which was noticed when smoke appeared from holes in the cliff face. The tunnels had been used for 25 years by the George Hammond company for storage and contained 2,000 wooden pallets. Up to 100 firemen and 12 pumps were used, but firemen could only work for short periods due to the terrific heat, which reached 800° centigrade. It took 28 hours to put out the fire. Tramps were known to sleep inside but nobody was found. Parts of the caves are still used for storage and workshops.

Further up the cliff face above them is a large U-shaped tunnel 10 (3m) to 12 feet (3.6m)

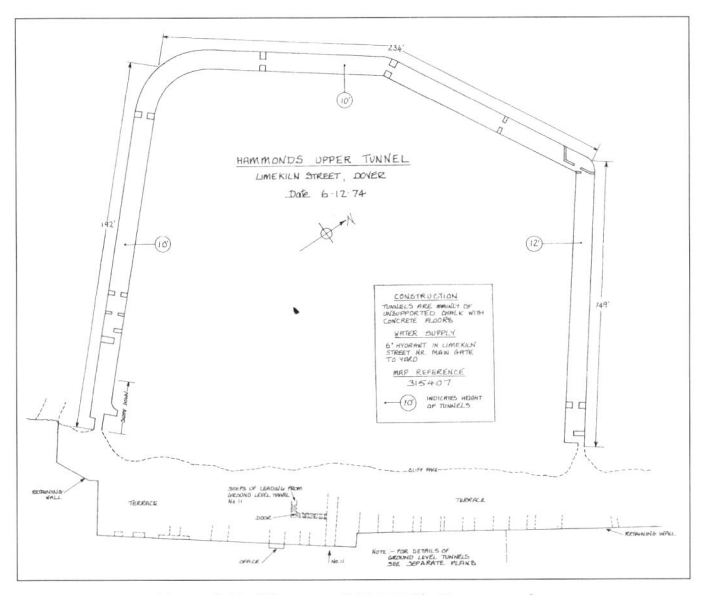

(Pic. 93) Upper Oil Mill Caves plan

high, known as Upper Oil Mills Cave, which was also used as an air raid shelter. Blast walls survive. It penetrates 190 feet (57m) into the cliff before running parallel to the cliff face for 234 feet (70m) and then returning to the alternative cliff face entrance.

DOE Tunnels

This complicated set of tunnels, east of the Oil Mill Caves, were at the rear of the Dover Storage Company in the 1970s and are now at the

(Pics. 94, 95) Oil Mill Caves

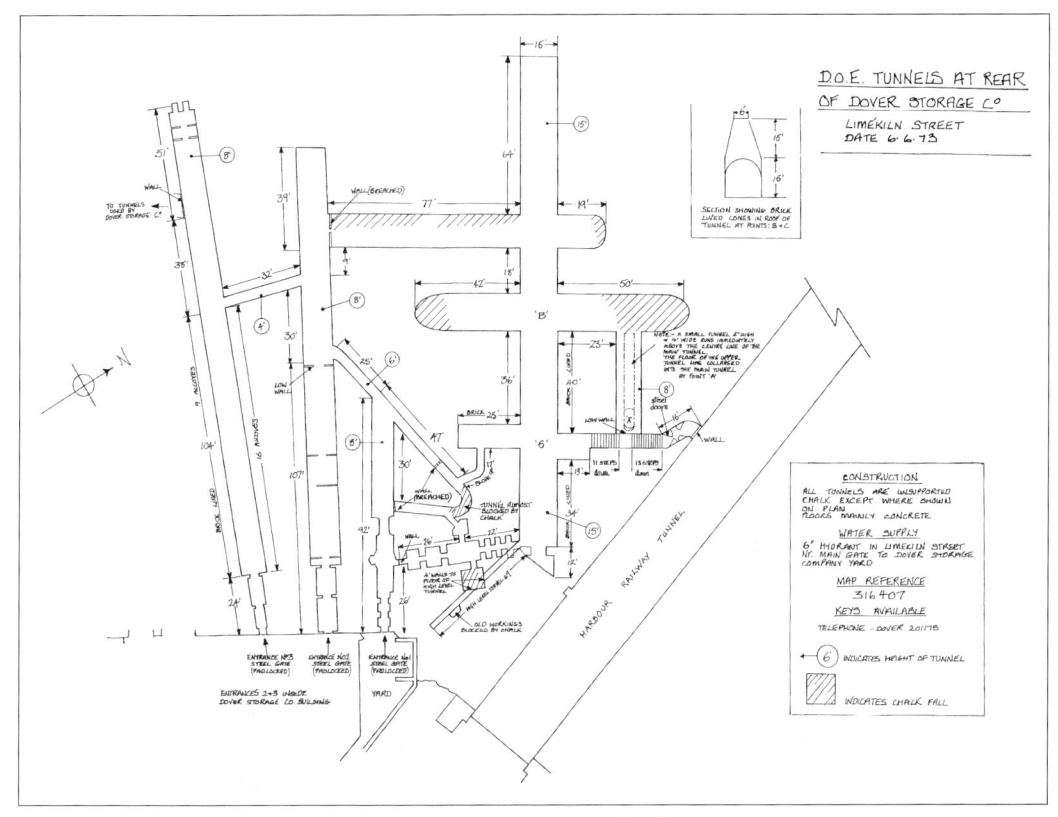

(Pic. 96) DOE Tunnels plan

rear of Folkestone Fixings. Since they are known as the DOE tunnels, they were presumably owned at some time post Second World War by the Department of the Environment. Probably excavated in the early 19th century originally, there is evidence of use ever since, including as an air raid shelter during the Second World War. A stairway apparently built at this time links it to the adjacent railway tunnel. The brickwork is impressive in the main section. John Walton recorded that at the western end are three interconnected tunnels penetrating almost 200 feet (60m) with brick-lined alcoves on both sides. This set is connected to yet another complex penetrating 160 feet (48m) from the railway tunnel. Remains of

(Pic. 97) DOE Tunnels "dome"

(Pic. 98) DOE Tunnels

some older collapsed tunnels at a slightly higher level are visible. Graffiti dated 1905 survive. It is rumoured that a secret railway platform existed in the Priory Tunnel for the discharge of wounded and dead servicemen into the DOE tunnels, although this is unlikely considering their use as an air raid shelter.

Dover Priory/Harbour railway tunnel

In 1989 Harold Sneller and David Burridge, accompanied by the Dover Priory station master, walked into the Priory railway tunnel under the Western Heights when the line was closed. They entered a short passage 10 feet (3m) long and 5 feet (1.4m) wide off the side of the tunnel leading to a room 20 feet (6m) square with a brick barrel-vaulted roof, partly dismantled fireplace and chimney. Between the room and the railway tunnel were two smaller rooms 10 feet (3m) square side by side and end on to the tunnel, each having two slits for rifle fire. Brickwork seemed to be the same age as the main tunnel – 1861. The explanation for this is that when the London, Chatham and Dover Railway Company sought permission from the War Department to extend the railway from Priory Station through the Western Heights cliffs (owned by the Ordnance Department) to the Pier District, a condition was that it should be fortified at the company's expense. This was to be a casemated battery over the tunnel to command the line with an underground connection between the battery and the Grand Shaft staircase 300 feet (90m) away. At this time there was fear of a French invasion with military improvements in progress at both the Western Heights and the Castle to make the port of Dover impregnable from attack by land or sea. During this visit, however, there was no sign of any battery above the tunnel or a connection to the Grand Shaft, which may never have been built.

One of the small rooms was used as an emergency centre during the Second World War and clerical staff would move in for short periods during emergencies to carry on with their work. When shelling started somebody recalled carrying a heavy typewriter for the lady railway clerk through the railway tunnel to the rooms so that she could carry on typing!

Packet Yard Well

The Packet Yard that was in Snargate Street (to the east of the Priory Tunnel) and owned by the railway company was used for repair work on the railway ferries. Packet Yard Well is a misnomer, but named so in the 1970s by John Walton and his fire service colleagues as it was only 12 feet (3.6m) to the east of the Packet Yard boundary. With a diameter of 4 feet (1.2m) in diameter, it reached water 20 feet (6m) down. With road widening since then, it is probably now under the A20 or demolished. Its purpose is not known, but was probably not a source of drinking water so close to sea water.

Scott's Caves/Snargate Tunnels West

Situated to the west of the Grand Shaft these tunnels were referred to as Scott's Caves in the 1950s when a national register was compiled of underground caves and tunnels suitable for use as nuclear shelters during the Cold War. Scott's was a well known dyer and cleaning firm

(Pic. 99) Scotts Caves

that closed in 1963. Here two main parallel tunnels or vaulted chambers are connected by smaller spur tunnels. One of the tunnels after 175 feet (54m) ends at a shaft. The shaft is 8 feet (2.5m) in diameter and reaches the cliff top after 120 feet (36m). It is thought to have been a well at one time for the Grand Shaft Barracks above, but it was converted during the Second World War as an escape shaft when one tunnel was used as an air raid shelter and the other as a naval workshop. Scott's, who had premises in front of these tunnels for many years made use of them as engineering workshops. When John Walton surveyed them in the 1970s, long after Scott's had disappeared, he found a dry cleaning machine in one.

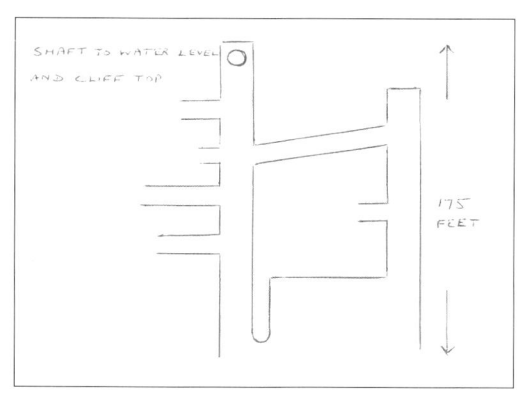

(Pic. 100) Sketch of Scotts Caves

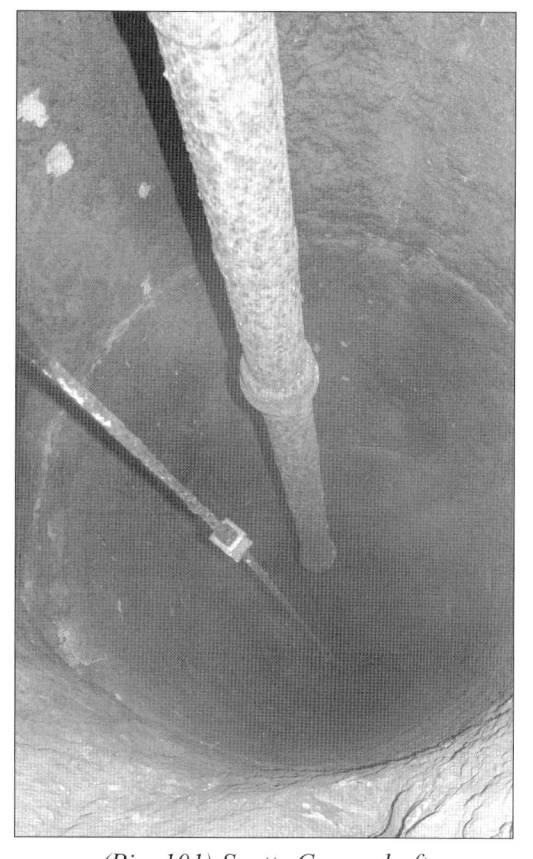

Snargate Street tunnels

This complex comprises Barwicks (formerly Courts and now Bluebirds), Crouchers (now Ardee Hose) and Motel (formerly the Shaftesbury Hotel and Soldiers' Home). During the Second World War a connecting tunnel was dug to form a large complex of air raid shelters. At the same time a long tunnel was excavated under Cowgate Cemetery which connected these tunnels with Durham Hill, but in 1943 a shell penetrated it and blocked it. Graffiti evidence survives. Most are lined with brick or concrete but some are unsupported chalk.

Barwicks (now Bluebirds) Caves

Apparently these caves with three entrances in Snargate Street were excavated in the early nineteenth century for wine merchant Stephen Court at the rear of his premises and for many years were known as Court's Caves. Stephen Court also constructed terraced gardens on the cliffs above complete with a folly. The tunnels are lined throughout with alcoves for wine storage. The maximum penetration is 170 feet (51m) with a maximum height and width of 10 feet (3m). When owned by Barwicks, the building firm, they were used as a store. When visited a few years ago part was being used to store uniforms, equipment and props for war films.

(Pic. 101) Scotts Caves shaft

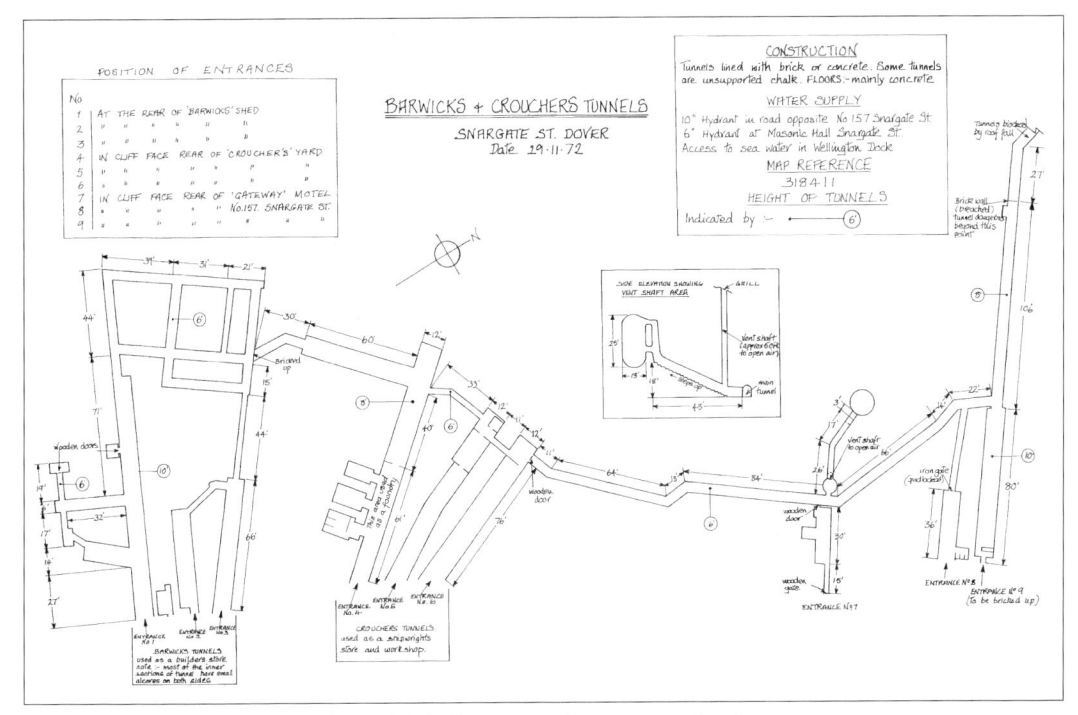

(Pic. 102) Snargate Street tunnels plan

(Pic. 103) Snargate Street tunnels

Croucher's (now Ardee Hose) Tunnels

Herbert Croucher, shipwright, owned these tunnels at 141 Snargate Street in 1971. Tunnels with three entrances penetrate up to 100 feet (30m) and are connected to each other at the rear by a 70 feet (21m) long tunnel. In 1972 the first 60 feet (18m) of the first tunnel was being used as a foundry. A 90 feet (27m) long tunnel running to the west connected with Barwick's Caves although it is now bricked up.

Motel (formerly Soldiers' Home and Shaftesbury Hotel) tunnels, Snargate Street

This set has three entrances behind the recently demolished motel. The first tunnel (going east) penetrates 45 feet (13.5m) to a connecting tunnel which runs both east and west. Going straight on, however, immediately there is a 50 feet (15m) high ventilation shaft followed by 46 steps to a large circular chamber, thought to be a limekiln, 13 feet (4m) in diameter and 25 feet (7.5m) high. The connecting tunnel running to the west reaches a gate blocking further access after 148 feet (44m). Eastwards it reaches the tunnels from the other two entrances after 100 feet (30m). The tunnel from the final entrance penetrates over 200 feet (60m) before becoming blocked by a roof fall.

Winchelsea Caves

Away from the coast and into the town, there is a maze of tunnels off the Folkestone Road known as the Winchelsea Caves with entrances in the former Winchelsea quarry. They were excavated at least in part by REs as tunnelling practice to construct shelters for civilians during the First World War. Later, a Dover Borough Council minute, dated September 1918, agreed that a letter be sent to the Officer Commanding the Dover Garrison thanking the REs for excavating a tunnel shelter between the Winchelsea and Tower Hamlets chalk pits. The

(Pic. 104) Snargate Street tunnels   *(Pic. 105) Winchelsea Caves*

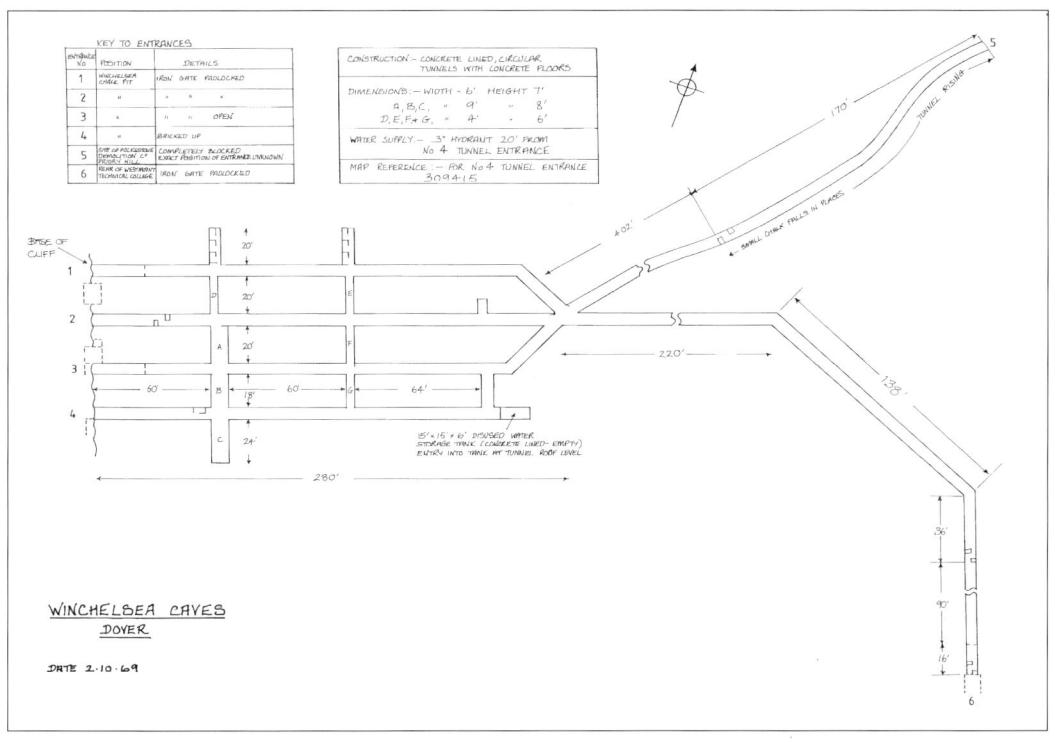

(Pic. 106) Winchelsea Caves plan

(Pic. 107) Winchelsea Caves

REs used a boring machine that could cut 60 feet (18m) a day. The concrete-lined circular tunnels reflect the use of the boring machine. Having proved its worth, it was then moved to France for use in Flanders at Hill 60 a few miles SE of Ypres, a German observation post overlooking the Allied front. In 1915 171 Tunnelling Company dug into the hill, laid mines and blew it up. The Winchelsea Caves were used again as a shelter during the Second World War. There were four entrances with blast barriers leading to rough-dug and lined tunnels that could house 1000 people. Whilst at one time people could walk all the way through to Tower Hamlets or to Westmount, now the Winchelsea end is used for storage by an engineering company, but the tunnel is blocked halfway. Explorers have found the remains of a possible mustard gas decontamination centre close to the entrance. A water tank and toilet cubicles are still there as well as marks where three-tiered bunks once stood and a kitchen sink in the canteen area. An explosion in the 1980s during construction work was apparently caused by cutting through cables that had been live for 40 years.

John Walton's plan, drawn in the 1970s, records four entrance tunnels penetrating 174 feet (52m) before converging and giving a choice of routes. A left fork leads to an exit on Priory Hill after 600 feet (180m). The section going straight on, after a couple of turns, ends after some 238 feet (71m) at the rear of Westmount on Folkestone Road.

Castlemount Road

Behind Castlemount Road houses are or were a complex of tunnels used as an air raid shelter, but much older than the Second World War. It has been suggested that these tunnels reach as far as the castle walls and were dug by French soldiers besieging the castle in 1216.

Blackman's (formerly Beaufoy's) Cave, Lagoon Cave and Tower Hamlets Road tunnel

Behind Blackman's in the High Street is a (blocked) entrance to a tunnel which goes under the back garden of a Priory Hill house and then into a chalk wall. *The Dover Express* in 1993 reported that a Priory Hill property owner used to receive a shilling a year rent from the Board of Trade to use the tunnel. Turning right at the entrance another tunnel runs nearly 225 feet (67m) behind High Street shops, meeting a 165 feet (50m) long tunnel from an entrance/exit to the rear of where Lagoon Garage once stood. The connecting tunnel then runs for 246 feet (74m) to Tower Hamlets Road with another entrance. Prewar the Blackman's and Lagoon Caves were entirely separate, but apparently in order to make them safe as air raid shelters the connecting tunnel was dug and completed with a semicircular, arched roof lined with concrete and a concrete floor.

An explorer described his progress from the entrance in Tower Hamlets Road to the Lagoon Cave: 'The main tunnel descends rapidly from

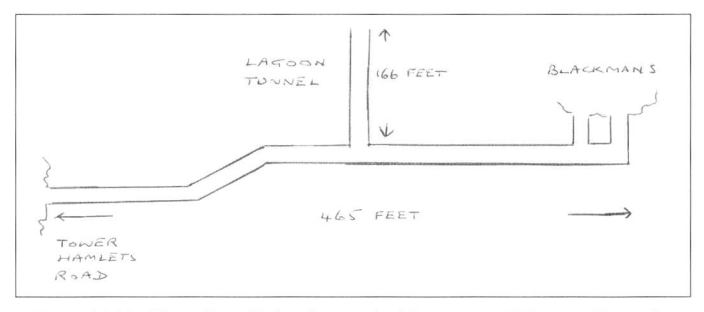

(Pic. 108) Sketch of Blackman's / Lagoon / Tower Hamlets Caves

(Pic. 109) Lagoon Cave

(Pic. 110) Tower Hamlets Tunnel

the entrance, twisting and turning as we progressed through. Like the Noah's Ark Tunnel, there are short spurs every 100 yards (90m) or so which were used for toilets. About two thirds of the way along the tunnel's length it was blocked and the section beyond backfilled with builders' rubbish. A separate tunnel branches off the main section towards another street entrance. Unlike other long air raid tunnels, this system is protected by blast walls along its length. It terminates in a small tiled kitchen area and toilet block with the street level entrance on the right hand side. It was quite weird standing there listening to diners in the restaurant immediately above.'

Noah's Ark Tunnel

This tunnel, which runs from Noah's Ark Road to Coombe Valley Road, existed by 1939 to carry a water main, but was converted to shelter 800

(Pic. 111) Noah's Ark Tunnel graffiti

people. Opened to visitors for a day in 2010, it is in good condition. Entering from Noah's Ark Road by a short flight of steps it is basically a long straight tunnel about 1100 feet (330m) long, 5 feet (1.5m) wide and 7 feet (2m) high. At the midway point the tunnel is some 100 feet (30m) below the top of the hill above. Concrete-lined with a kitchen area, toilets and three sets of blast walls, some wartime graffiti survive. There would have been bunk beds down one side and benches on the other. There are still some numbers on the wall to identify sleepers' allotted space. A newspaper report stated that Margaret Amos carried furniture through it to her first home.

Buckland Hospital tunnel

Behind the hospital a Second World War air raid shelter was constructed comprising shuttered, concrete-lined tunnels which formed a rectangle. A connecting tunnel apparently led to a similar second part.

Buckland public air raid shelter

In Union Road, now Coombe Valley Road, beside Buckland Hospital and now used as a car park, was an underground public air raid shelter. Jon Iveson recalled looking round it some 20 years ago. Presumably a cut and cover construction, it comprised two rectangular chambers with connecting tunnels.

Regent Cinema cave shelter

As part of the Second World War air raid precautions a cave shelter was excavated behind the Regent (later Odeon) Cinema in London Road the site of which is now occupied by the Territorial Army Centre. Lined with timber and with a cinder floor, it could accommodate 160 people, but in 1954 a retaining wall was constructed blocking the two entrances.

School underground air raid shelters

With the threat of invasion and danger from air raids, most of Dover's 3,000 school children were evacuated in 1940 to South Wales. As the threat of invasion receded many youngsters returned to Dover to join the 800 who never left. There was a need for schools to reopen, but apparently they could only do so if there was adequate air raid protection. Many school shelters were built on low budgets, some little more than reinforced rooms, others purpose-built, but usually merely cut and cover trenches. Those schools occupied during the war by the armed services, such as the two grammar schools, also had extensive underground shelters provided.

Christchurch Tunnel

Christchurch tunnel was a Second World War air raid shelter from Bowling Green Terrace to the playground of Christchurch School on North Military Road. From the Bowling Green Terrace entrance the tunnel runs straight for 120 feet (37m) before turning at right angles. After another 75 feet (23m) there is a T-junction with both ways leading to exit/entrances. Whilst the first 188 feet (58m) are concrete-lined the remainder is chalk with timber roof supports.

Dover Girls' Grammar School

An extensive cut and cover air raid shelter still exists at Dover Girls' Grammar School under the tennis courts. Presumably the shelter was not constructed for the school as it was evacuated to South Wales during the Second World War and did not reopen in Dover until 1945. It is thought that WRNS occupied the school. There are

(Pic. 112) Christchurch Tunnel

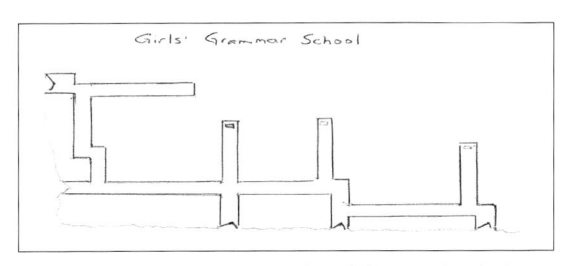

(Pic. 113) Grammar School for Girls shelter

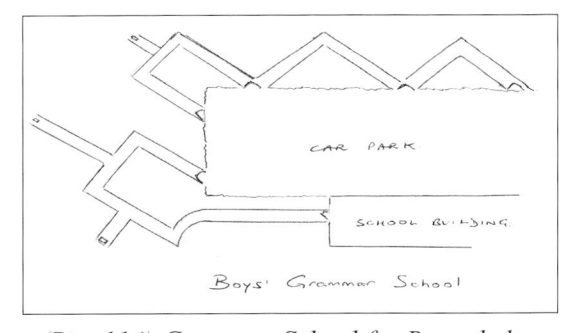

(Pic. 114) Grammar School for Boys shelter

five entrances plus three manhole covers, which could also be used for escape if necessary. The complex comprises a connecting tunnel of some 170 feet (50m) running parallel with the bank with three 33 feet (10m) tunnels branching off it into the bank and another 81 feet (25m) long ending at one of the entrances.

Dover Boys' Grammar School

Dover Boys' Grammar School or County School as it was called until the end of the Second World War was also occupied by the WRNS during the war. There still exists around the present day car park by the main school entrance a complex set of underground tunnels used as air raid shelters; almost all are interconnected and were constructed presumably for the service personnel. There are six entrances, including one within the school, and three escape shafts each 3 feet (1m) in diameter with vertical steel ladders.

Astor School tunnel

Apparently some people can remember playing in a tunnel somewhere behind the old Astor School site (now housing called Auden Way) which ran to Priory Hill where there was a First World War air raid shelter in the chalk pit, but no other details have come to light.

Other school shelters

Underneath the playground of the former Buckland School in London Road there is a wartime air raid shelter. Two stepped entrances lead

(Pic. 115) Dover Grammar School for Girls shelter

(Pic. 116) Charlton Shelter

down to a complex of tunnels 6 feet 6 inches (2m) high and 5 feet (1.5m) wide. Two parallel tunnels some 80 feet (23m) long are connected by four tunnels 40 feet (11.5m) long. One of the long tunnels could lead to further tunnels but a chalk collapse prevents exploration. Similar shelters, which survive, were provided under the playgrounds of Charlton and St. Martin's Schools. Barton Road School had air raid shelters which were entered at playground level but were below the adjoining Barton Road road level. The school also has a 'proper' tunnel beside the school that runs parallel with the The Grove houses for about 60 feet (18m). After a couple of bends it ends with three toilets.

Dover Waterworks

Looking at the magnificent engine house of the former Dover Waterworks on Connaught Road, there is no indication of what lies beneath. In order to supply mains water to the town two wells over 200 feet (60m) deep were sunk. At their foot tunnels, one 200 feet (60m) long, led to two separate springs. Pipe tunnels carried the water to an underground reservoir 108 feet (32m) by 24 feet (7m) able to hold 500,000 gallons. This reservoir with its impressive 15 Gothic arches supporting the roof was used at the opening in 1853 as a banqueting hall for 100 people – all male. Two pumps could lift up to 55,000 gallons of water an hour, but demand soon outstripped supply and in 1862 a second lower reservoir with a capacity of one million gallons was constructed. This required another 300 feet (90m) of tunnelling to reach

(Pic. 117) Waterworks Reservoir

(Pic. 118) Waterworks Reservoir

the springs and with a third pump installed in 1882 75,000 gallons an hour could be raised. A shaft with winding steps provided access first to the lower reservoir and then to a pipe tunnel. A third reservoir was constructed in 1940.

East Cliff Caves

Returning to the seafront and the cliffs, in the 1800s it was said that every house in East Cliff backing onto the cliffs had its own cave. Some years ago a vast chamber in the chalk was found previously concealed by a concrete garage. Barry Stock claimed that 'Napoleonic prisoners had been held there for up to two years and to while away the time they had carved the ceiling into the most amazing relief scenes – it was quite magical.'

The major caves at the foot of the East Cliff, which are also known as Esplanade Level (of the castle), comprise the fascinating Trevanion, Chapel and Athol Terrace Caves plus the connecting Guilford Tunnel. Privately owned before the war they are now in the care of English Heritage as part of its Dover Castle property.

Guilford Tunnel

This tunnel, constructed during the Second World War, is over 1300 feet (390m) long and connects the Trevanion, Chapel and Athol Terrace caves. It is mainly unlined chalk with some brick pillars.

Trevanion Caves

This labyrinth of tunnels with five entrances of unlined chalk supported in places by brick arches is bounded inland by the Guilford Tunnel. A high level water tank survives.

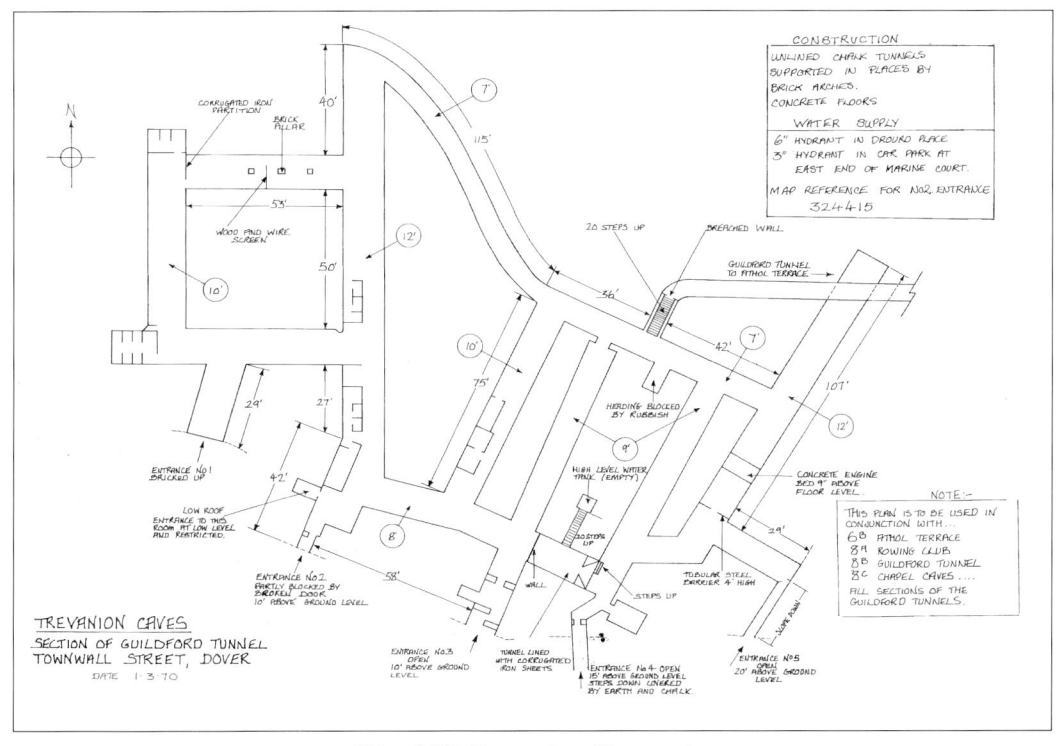

(Pic. 119) Trevanion Caves plan

Medieval carvings are said to exist in these caves, but the origins are unknown. They were almost certainly used by smugglers and were certainly used as air raid shelters. In 1959 part was being used by Arthur Liddon, a boatman, as a workshop to make lobster pots.

Chapel Caves

Situated between Trevanion Street and Athol Terrace cave systems, the Chapel Caves are mainly unlined chalk with concrete floors. There are two entrances; one gives immediately onto a cavern-like cave with two sections 27 feet (8m) and 17 feet (5m) long from which the caves

(Pic. 120) Trevanion Caves

get their name. This cavern is connected to another complex of tunnels that penetrates about 50 feet (15m) with its own entrance. Steps connect with the Guilford Tunnel.

Athol Terrace

These caves were apparently rediscovered by some boys in 1891. Well known Dovorian, Joe Harman, recalled that in about 1927 Dover Corporation bought the stonemason's and sweet shop next to the Bull Inn at Buckland Bridge to widen

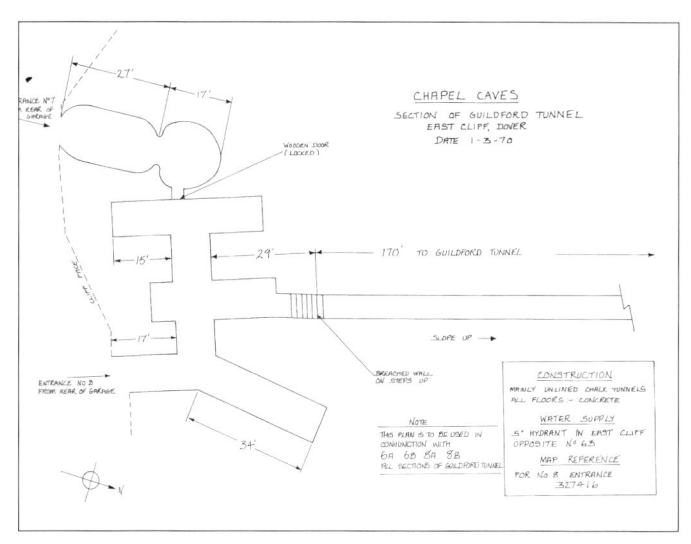

(Pic. 121) Chapel Caves plan

the bridge. George Small, who kept the sweet shop, moved his shop to the bottom of the cliff adjoining Athol Terrace, converting a building into a cafe and opening up the caves behind, charging 3d a time to view. Extremely complex to describe, these tunnels are mainly rough chalk supported in places by brick or concrete pillars. Originally there were four entrances leading to different parts of the complex, penetrating up to 150 feet (45m) and connected to the Guilford Tunnel during the Second World War.

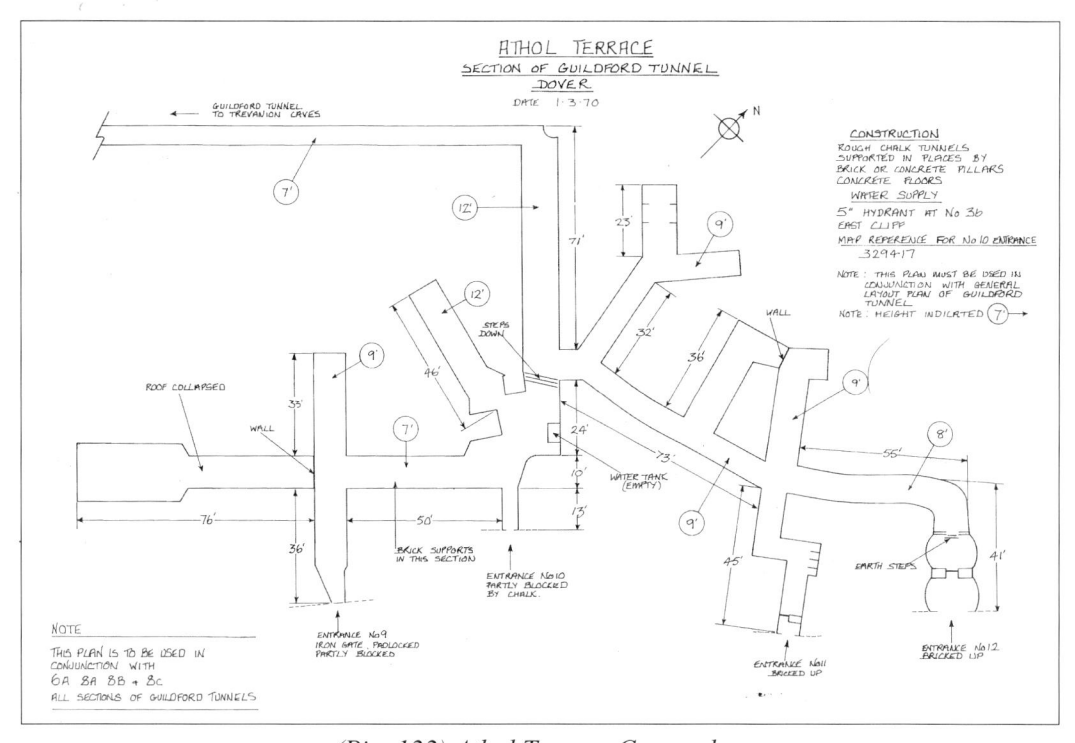

(Pic. 122) Athol Terrace Caves plan

(Pic. 123) Athol Terrace shop

(Pic. 124) Athol Terrace Caves

Cave dwellers

The construction of Dover's Admiralty Harbour in the years before and after 1900 cut back hundreds of yards of the eastern cliff face, obliterating all trace of a recent troglodyte (cave dwelling) culture. Some of these caves were used for storage whilst others were lived in. One set of caves had grand church-like entrances with Gothic arched windows known as The Grotto, part of which still exist as the Chapel Caves (see above). Two sketches by John Natte (c1765-1822) show details of three separate structures including a two-storeyed entrance approached by steps cut into the chalk. Above the middle open door a number of dovecotes can be seen and there is a ladder to assist the collection of gulls' eggs – a delicacy apparently. The Grotto was built to house John Smith's stone coffin, but was not used at his death as his sons chose to bury him in a conventional churchyard. Close by, John Smith had built in 1791 the first substantial house at East Cliff (close to today's entrance to the Eastern Docks). It comprised a two storey, castellated building with an entrance flanked by two round towers. There was also a separate tower with a spire and six outbuildings whose roofs were upturned boats. This strange architecture was expensive for a relatively poor residence. No wonder it soon became known as Smith's Folly.

The 1841 census records caves on this cliff being lived

(Pic. 125) John Natte's 'Grotto in the Cliffs'

(Pic. 126) East Cliff cave cottage

(Pic. 127) Interior of cave cottage

in by James Hart and his family and by widow Mary Burville and her four children. In the 1851 census Mary Burville was still there with her daughter Elizabeth; both were recorded as laundresses. Cave homes were easily extended by excavating yet more chalk. A watercolour by W. H. Prior in about 1850 shows a cave dwelling with a chimney, three windows and a door. Chalk blocks formed the boundary walls and possibly kept the pigs in! It is thought that pigs were kept in caves as well as smuggled goods, which were wrapped in oilskins and hidden in barrels of pig manure to deceive the excise men!

Hanvey's Tunnel

An 1876 Dover Guide mentions a tunnel from Athol Terrace to the cliff top built in 1870 by the Chamber of Commerce and supervised by John Hanvey, Borough Surveyor, which provided a short cut to the beach and castle compared with the road from Deal over the downs. A man was employed at 2s 6d a week to sweep the tunnel path and to prevent disorderly conduct such as boys yelling at the top of the tunnel frightening people ascending! The cutting back of the cliff face when the Admiralty Harbour was built obliterated all trace of the tunnel.

Aerial ropeway tunnels

Incensed at the charges of the Southern Railway to carry coal from his mine at Tilmanstone to the docks at Dover, Richard Tilden Smith decided to construct an aerial ropeway 7.5 miles (11km) long from Tilmanstone to the Eastern Docks at Dover to carry up to 120 tons of coal an hour in buckets holding 14.5 cwts. To achieve this twin tunnels 400 feet (120m) long were carved by Tilmanstone miners from Langdon Hole to a point above the Eastern Arm. The ropeway was completed in 1930, but was only operational for a short time and was eventually dismantled in 1950. The distinctive sealed exits from these tunnels in the cliff side can still be seen from the Eastern Arm.

(Pic. 128) Aerial Ropeway emerging through cliffs

(Pic. 129) Fan Bay Beach Chamber

(Pic. 130) Fan Bay Beach Chamber

Fan Bay Beach Shaft

Six feet (2m) above the beach at Fan Bay is an entrance to a tunnel 7 feet (2m) wide and 6 feet (2m) high and 13 feet (4m) long leading to a chamber 20 feet (6m) by 15 feet (4.5m) with a shaft 10 feet (3m) in diameter which reaches water at 25 feet (7.5m). Metal rungs go part way down acting as a ladder, but the purpose of this shaft and cave is a mystery. It could possibly have been a fisherman's cave and a metal door may have been taken from the 1910 wreck of the *Preussen* nearby.

There is, however, one known use of the cave. In March 1962 the *Kentish Express* reported that Antoni Nowacki, a 43 years old Pole, was arrested at Fan Bay and charged under the Vagrancy Act. A policeman had to make a hazardous descent down the cliff face to make the arrest and found the man in a bunk said to be 30 feet (9m) from the cliff face. Apparently, the floor of the man-made cave was only just above high water mark. The Pole had repeatedly refused to go to a reception centre for vagrants. Sentencing the man to three months in prison, the magistrate stated that the prisoner 'was going against the laws of the land by living in caves.'

Canterbury Cave

Canterbury Cave is thought to be a natural cave, part of a fossil cave system eroded by marine action and is situated to the west of St. Margaret's Bay beyond Ness Point and above high tide level. There is a passage 7 feet (2m) wide and 4 feet (1m) high that goes into the cliff face for 80 feet (24m) before turning in to a chamber 30 feet (9m) by 12 feet (3m) by 5 feet (1.5m) high. Fifty yards (46m) further on the passage becomes a flat crawl for 20 feet (6m) before reaching a

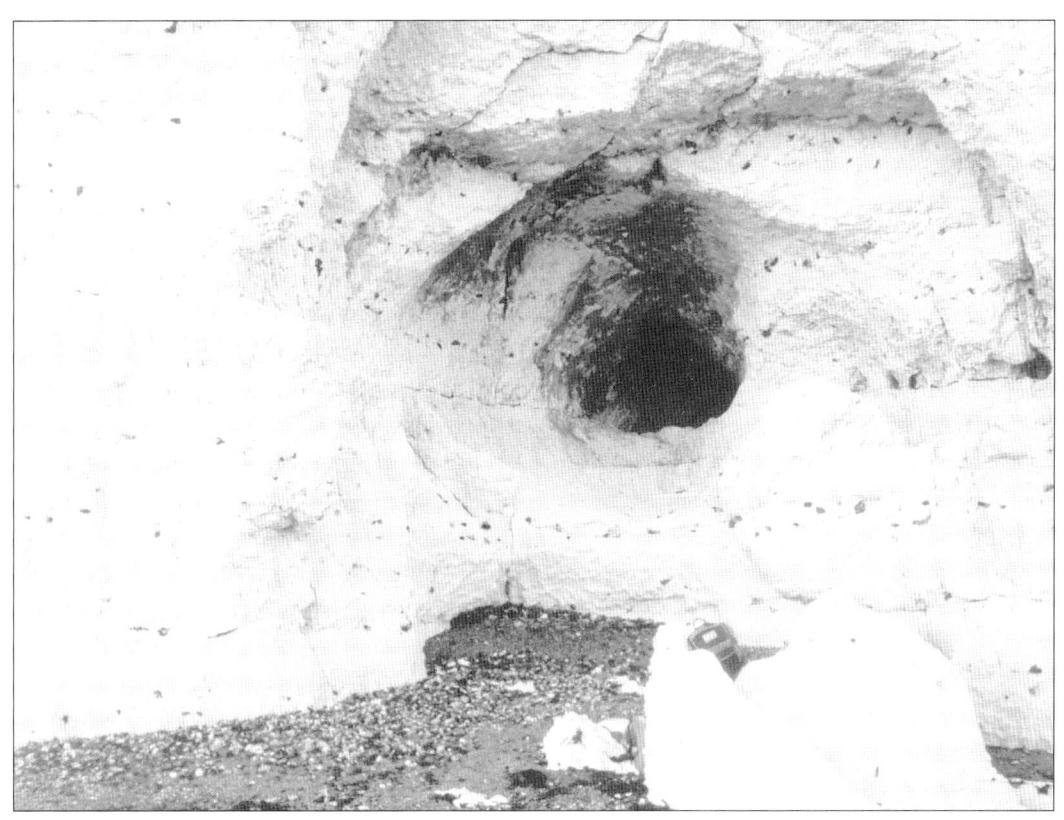

(Pic. 131) Canterbury Cave

T junction. When explored in 1976 by the Chelsea Spelealogical Society and T. Reeve the roof and walls were covered in scallop markings and both flints and fossils protruded from the chalk. At floor level were several tube-like openings up to 9 inches (7cm) in diameter. After yet another 70 feet (21m) crawling over large boulders there was another roomier passage that continued for 500 feet (150m) before being blocked by chalk rubble.

Bay Hill, St. Margaret's

In 2004 a garden shed at Bay Hill, St Margaret's was removed revealing some brickwork. Carved over an archway was a shield with a Fleur de Lis and the date 1855. A vaulted brick tunnel was unearthed leading across the road to South Sands House.

Granville Hotel site and others St. Margaret's Bay

At the foot of the cliff at St. Margaret's Bay are a number of small caves, which were at the rear of the dwellings that once faced the seashore and were presumably used for storage. Further up the cliff some houses made use of existing or excavated new caves to act as air raid shelters during the Second World War. The Granville Hotel on Hotel Road (Granville Apartments now occupies the site) had its own cave shelters. Since the hotel was occupied by the army during the war, its caves may well have been excavated for their use. When the building reverted to hotel use the caves were apparently used to dump empty bottles - before the days of recycling.

Guston

Underneath a cottage in Guston is a mysterious well shaft. From the cellar of the cottage steps lead to a brick-lined tunnel some 40 feet (11.5m) long and 7 feet (2m) wide. Off this tunnel is another 40 feet (11.5m) passage leading to a well shaft of unlined chalk 252 feet (75m) deep to water level.

(Pic. 132) Guston Mystery Cave

Chapter 2
First World War Caves, Tunnels and Shelters

Following the outbreak of war in August 1914 the 43,645 Dovorians became involved in a continental war that past generations had never experienced with German bombing raids and destroyers trying to shell the town. Dover gained the doubtful honour of being the first town in England to be bombed. On Christmas Eve, 1914 a 14 lb (6kg) bomb was dropped from a German aircraft and landed in a garden, knocking a man off his ladder but with little other damage. By 1918 bombs could weigh 3,000lbs (1364kg).

In January 1916 a joint statement was issued by Mayor Farley and the Garrison Commander that after the siren warning people should take cover in the nearest house, preferably the cellar. In fact they were more likely to go out of their houses to see the air raid! Schools had no shelters. During 1916 nine civilian lives were lost in air raids – the first attacks on the town causing loss of life since 1294. In May 1916 the Amusements Committee of the Borough Council approved the loan of chairs for use during air raids in the Trevanion Caves and a cave owned by J. W. Bussey & Co. in Northampton Street. From July 1916 Mr Grimer, the owner of the Trevanion Caves at the foot of Castle Cliff, urged the town council

(Pic. 133) Pier Infants

(Pic. 134) Chitty's Mill

to take over his caves and control the use of them as shelters. In September he offered to surrender his lease to the Corporation as he was unwilling to be responsible any longer for supervising their use. As a result the Mayor asked the Dover Chief Constable to provide a police constable when the caves were occupied. Civilians were not safe. Many worked for the military and in the naval dockyard and so Admiral Bacon agreed to the use of the Trevanion Caves by civilians as air raid shelters. Initially people were urged to dig their own shelters and some with properties backing on to the cliffs did so, but from September 1917 new air raid shelters were built in parts of the town remote from cave shelters, including those at Chapel Hill, Mayfield Avenue, the Steam Laundry, Tower Hamlets, Monins Rd, Westbury Rd, Castlemount and Bunkers Hill.

(Pic. 135) Trevanion Caves

(Pic. 136) Oil Mill Caves

More than £1500 had already been spent in constructing shelters and the committee had authorised the temporary employment for two weeks at 25 shillings a week of a cleaner at the County School for Boys. The construction of additional shelters was recommended at Bunker's Hill, Glenfield Road, Heathfield Avenue, Westmount, Belgrave Road, Clarendon Place and Astley Avenue. Also recommended was another urgent appeal for voluntary labour to help with construction, to request civilian use of the Army Pay Corps Offices dug-out at night and for notices to be displayed in the shelters warning people not to drink, smoke or swear!

Prior to air raid shelters being constructed existing caves were the primary shelters. Thirty feet (9m) of chalk above shelters or caves was considered safe. There was a nightly pilgrimage to the caves – a long procession of women, youngsters and old men from all directions with perambulators or handcarts loaded with mattresses, pillows, blankets, food baskets and girls carrying dolls. People from the heavily populated Pier District went to the Oil Mill caves which could hold thousands. They were broad and lofty chambers leading from one to another and well-ventilated. Inside were benches on all sides and electric lights. Separate caves opened off the main cave for men, women and children. Soldiers and constables patrolled, keeping excellent order. Other caves under the Castle, which were bomb proof and almost sound proof, were reserved for servicemen and their families. Storage vaults under the Phoenix Brewery and even the Priory/Harbour railway tunnel were used. Two sets of caves at the back of High Street were used as was the Grand Shaft. Up to 800 people used the basement and the police cells under the Town Hall.

In the book, *The Life and Times of a Dovorian*, Lillian Kay, who was born in 1914 and lived in the Pier District of Dover, remembered, 'When there was any trouble the "syreen" went, I was wrapped up in a blanket, and then we all rushed to the caves in the cliffs off Limekiln Street. Our cave was just behind where the petrol station is now. We stayed all night sometimes with our own bedding on the floor with about ten other families. There were plenty of caves to use. When the war was over we went to get our bedding from the caves. I was dreadfully upset that we were never going to sleep with our pals again. I still have a poem called 'A Night in the Oil Caves' by F.B.Spice; it is printed on a single sheet of paper, priced one penny and is dated October 6th 1917 – my mother must have bought it at the time. It captures the atmosphere in those makeshift shelters':

Into a cave with whitewashed walls
There are crowds of people stay
Women with babes, men, girls and boys
Just to be out of harm's way
For you don't hear much of the 'Syreen'
Nor yet the terrible guns,
Tho' you may hear the sound of rumbling
Perhaps of a falling bomb.

A Doctor sits at a table
With his wife and nurses fair,
To render first aid to those who might faint
Or taken in any way queer.
Then the 'Tommies' give boiling water
To those who like to make tea
Or Bovril or anything else they may want!
Why the time goes merrily.

The caves may be a bit draughty
But still we like to stay,
For no matter what may happen outside
We are safe out of danger's way.
In a nook you will see a mattress
With seven children sleeping there
Others you find are writing
Perhaps to the 'boys' over there.

Yes! Fighting for Country and Freedom
And the homes they love so dear.
We pray that the war will be ended
For them to have Christmas cheer.
And peace will be ours again.
We shall think of the nights that we spent from our homes
And the friends that we made at the caves.

In November 1917 a Corporation subcommittee was appointed to report on arrangements already made for air raid shelters and whether additional provision was desirable. It was also asked to report whether management committees were in place for every shelter and, if not, to appoint them. The committee reported later that month that the following public and private shelters had been or were being provided:

Pier Infants' School	Sanitary Steam Laundry
Viaduct Arch	Mannering's Mill
Viaduct Spur	Bradley's Stores
Caves at Oil Mill Barracks	Lloyd's Bank
Grand Shaft	Archcliffe Fort
Guard Room, North Military Road	Army Pay Corps Offices, Buckland
Sailors' and Soldiers' Home	Mr Wakefield's, Priory Hill
Finnis's Hill	Scott's Dye Works
Leney's Brewery	Hare & Hounds Hill
Leney's Mineral Water Factory	Dover Priory
Navy and Army Canteen Stores	Palmer's Carriage Works
Dover Engineering Works	Trevanion Caves
Burlington Hotel	Chitty's Mill
R.E. Caves (ie Winchelsea)	Beaufoy's Cave
Bussey's Caves, Northampton Street	Military Hill (near Christ Church)
Police Station	Military Hill (behind Clarendon Place)
School of Art	Markland Road
Town Hall Crypt	Widred Road
Pepper's Cave, 49 High Street	Chapel Hill
Connaught Park	Tower Hamlets Chalk Pit
Jam Stores, Bridge Street	St. Radigund's Road
County School for Boys	Co-operative Stores, River
Crabble Railway Arch	Maxton Brewery

Some Dovorians spent Christmas night 1917 in the caves. By the end of 1917 25,000 shelter places were available of one sort or another. One consequence was the loss of most trees from parks and roads to provide timber to support tunnel roofs. Relief finally came on Whit Sunday 1918 when the last air raid occurred.

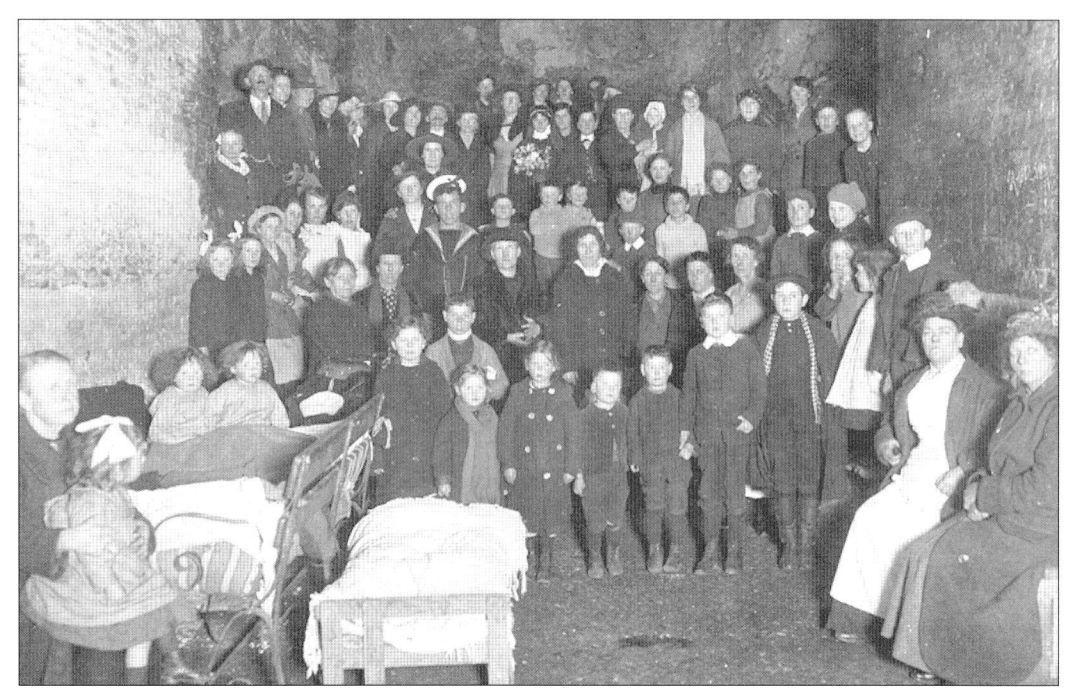

(Pic. 137) Sheltering in the caves

(Pic. 138) Evidence of tunnel boring machine in Winchelsea Caves

Chapter 3
Second World War Caves, Tunnels and Shelters

Prewar

Dover Borough Council minutes provide details of the extensive precautions taken both before and during the Second World War for the protection of the townspeople in which caves and tunnels played a vital role. From 1935, it is clear that the council was well aware of the air-raid threat and conscientious in its preparations. Dover had long been aware of the threat of bombardment from air and sea, having experienced it during the First World War. With war clouds forming over Europe, the council appointed an air-raid precautions (ARP) committee, which, by 1936, was making regular reports to the full council, pre-empting national air raid precautions. Dover was one of the first towns in the country prepared to spend money on air raid precautions before the 1937 ARP Act. The town had one particularly useful asset: a significant number of caves that could be adapted as deep shelters from air raids. The most sensible and practical option was to reopen the tunnels and caves used during the First World War. These precautions caused an increase in rates, initially a halfpenny in the pound.

(Pic. 139) Tower Hamlets tunnel

(Pic. 140) Trevanion Caves   *(Pic. 144) Trevanion Caves*

The government also wanted movement of the public to be kept to a minimum. This obviously demanded significant provision of public shelters throughout the town, as well as the later provision of family Anderson and Morrison shelters. Shelters were only one aspect of the precautions – gas attacks were also threatened.

In 1937 the Trevanion Street Caves were the first to be taken over by the council from Henry Crundall at a rent of £20 a year. Later, Winchelsea, Snargate Street and Priory Hill caves were requisitioned. The Oil Mill and East Cliff caves were taken over temporarily, but were handed back in October 1938 after Chamberlain returned from Munich declaring 'peace in our time'. The owner of the Oil Mill caves claimed compensation for loss of his mushroom crop! Estimates for the adaptation of the Athol Terrace Caves and the Soldiers' Home Cave in Snargate Street were submitted.

The source of funding for ARP became a serious concern for all local government authorities and the lack of government funding affected the pace of construction of air raid shelters. By the end of the year, parliament was discussing another ARP Bill, which amongst other provisions, requested the submission of ARP schemes for approval and offered sizeable grants for approved air-raid expenses.

The council sent off its proposals, requesting specific advice as to the suitability of the caves for shelter purposes. Approval was received in the middle of September for the use of most caves, and preparing the borough for war began in earnest. It was also agreed that in places at relatively low risk of attack during wartime, schools should remain open, but have shelters constructed. In high risk areas, schools were to close during hostilities and provision made for evacuation or keeping children at home.

The existing facilities were put to the test during the Munich Crisis of 1938 and extra facilities were constructed as a matter of urgency, including trench shelters in grounds owned by the corporation at Connaught Park by the children's playground, Pencester Gardens and River Recreation Ground as well as on private ground with the consent of the owners and at the electricity works. People were encouraged to build garden trenches and instructions were published in the local papers on how to make a sound trench shelter. Instructions were issued to ensure these facilities were made permanent, but orders were later given that trenches dug during the emergency were to be filled in, as the cost of making them permanent was prohibitive, while the actual protection afforded was minimal. With the renewed threat of war the situation was reversed in April 1939 when trench shelters at Pencester Gardens, Connaught Park (accommodating 423), Dover College playing field and Union Road were concrete-lined and covered with two feet of earth. Doors, chemical closets and seating were also provided. The River Recreation Ground trenches, however, were filled in to allow sports to resume! Following the outbreak of war more trench shelters were constructed.

(Pic. 142) Upper Oil Mill   *(Pic. 143) Winchelsea Cave*

(Pic. 144) Durham Hill tunnel

Dover's Chief of Police was also responsible for the town's fire service. As part of the Civil Defence air raid precautions it was supplemented from 1938 by the recruitment of part-time unpaid volunteers into the Auxiliary Fire Service (AFS) that soon had bases spread around the town, including one of the caves on Finnis's Hill. Both the AFS and the town fire service were absorbed in 1941 into the National Fire Service (NFS).

The imminent threat of war motivated the public to take a more active interest in ARP. W. H. Bennett responded positively by drafting a comprehensive civilian defence scheme for the town. The centre piece of Bennett's scheme was the construction of approximately 10,000 yards (9km) of additional tunnelling, in the shape of two subterranean networks, providing sufficient bomb and gas proof accommodation for everyone in the town. These tunnels would accommodate the 30,000 or so people that the existing caves would not protect. The scheme envisaged nobody in the town being more than ten minutes from a shelter entrance. The tunnels would be 7ft (2m) wide, reinforced by steel rings of the sort used by the mining industry, with wooden boards woven behind them. The estimated cost of the entire project, including excavation, labour and carting away of spoil, was £100,000-£120,000, with a certain amount being deductible as the excavated chalk would be of use to various industries. The cost of lighting, sanitation and seating was estimated at £6,000.

Bennett's Proposed Tunnels

1) Cave west of railway to Winchelsea Road Chalk Pit
2) Top Cave to Dover College grounds
3) Winchelsea Chalk Pit to Priory Hill
4) Double Tunnel from Chalk Pit to Prospect Place
5) Prospect Place to Cricket Ground
6) Cricket Ground to Coupers Covert
7) Covert to St Peter's Church
8) Castle Hill Caves to a point 300 yards NE
9) From NE point (of 8) to Coastguard station
10) Base of NE point to Godwyne Road water works
11) From Water Works to Connaught Park
12) Connaught Park to Danes Recreation Ground
13) Danes Recreation Ground to hill on Stanhope Road
14) Stanhope Road to Shrubbery House
15) Shrubbery House to hillside on Watling Street
16) Shrubbery House to Buckland Valley Farm
17) Hillside on Watling Street to Whitfield Road
18) Two "insets" from Tower Hamlets to (3) and (4): 220 yards from railway bridge and 440 yards to top end of Astor Avenue

Bennett's proposal seems to have greatly influenced council thinking. By early 1939, the council decided that tunnels would be an effective solution to the problem of air raid shelter provision and were probably the best way of protecting the civilian population. In fact only six people are mentioned in the council records as dying in deep shelter accommodation as a result of enemy action and five of those had failed to get within the blast walls. Other kinds of shelter offered protection from splinters, shrapnel or incendiaries, but the biggest threat proved to be high explosives; no surface or shallow underground shelter could withstand a close impact from a bomb of that type.

The Borough Council minutes of 28 February 1939 record a need to provide 23,550 deep shelter places for the townsfolk. This was to be achieved by adapting existing caves, constructing tunnels and adapting suitable basements as well as providing light, bomb proof shelters in localities remote from tunnels or caves. Works already completed at the Oil Mills Caves would shelter 750. The building firm of R. Barwick was prepared to lease its caves in Snargate Street, used for storage, for £100 a year and C. E. Beaufoy, the owner of Beaufoy's Cave in the High Street was also willing to make it available, although it would need adapting, as would the Athol Terrace Caves, (owned by the War Department and leased to Mr

Small), the Chapel Cave, (managed by the agents Mowll and Mowll), Trevanion Street Caves, (owned by H. & H. E. Crundall), Lagoon Cave (owned by W. H. Grigg), and Winchelsea Caves (owned by W. Paramor and the Crundall firm). A full report was also given of suitable localities for new tunnels and other shelters together with cost estimates and numbers that could be accommodated.

BOROUGH OF DOVER AIR RAID PRECAUTIONS
20 February 1939

1. Trenches (already partly constructed)

Locality	Accommodation	Approximate Persons cost in £
Pencester Gardens	306	1,072
Dover College playing field Elms Vale Road	306	1,044
Union Road	464	1,543
Connaught Park	306	1,056
Astor Avenue	306	1,025
	1688	5,740

2. Existing caves (already partly adapted)

Locality	Accommodation Persons	Approx. Cover of earth in feet	Approx. cost £
Athol Terrace, East Cliff	1,000	25-145	180
Chapel Cave rear of 61 East Cliff	200	20-100	60
Trevanion Street	700	30-60	100
Lagoon Garage, High Street	200	20-45	50
Winchelsea to Priory Hill	1,350	30-100	350
35 High Street (Beaufoy)	100		30
	3,550		770

3. Proposed tunnels

Locality	Length in yards	Effective length	Capacity	Cover of earth	Approx. cost in £
1. Isolation Hospital to Corporation Depot Union Rd.	379	318	850	30-105 feet	7,960

2.	Branch from above to Edred Road	478	437	1,275	30-105	8,560
3.	St Radigunds Road opposite Beaufoy Road to top of Bunkers Hill	422	355	1,000	30-110	8,490
4.	Branch between (3) and (5) above	545	545	1,700	110-190	8,185
5.	St Radigund's Rd at junction with Barwick Rd. to Crabble Lane	670	590	1,650	30-190	12,000
6.	Military Rd above Christ Church School	409	328	900	30-160	8,600
7.	Pilgrims Way near London Road, Kearsney to Whitfield Hill above Woodside	976	864	2,500	30-190	18,000
8.	Branches from no.6 to Folkestone Rd and to York St./Chapel Place	685	510	1,600	30-160	20,550
9.	Trevanion St. Caves to Taswell St. and Laureston Place	850	700	2,100	30-150	25,500
10.	Green Lane to Frith Road	1,880	1,580	4,750	30-80	56,400
11.	Under Western Heights between Belgrave Rd and Folkestone Rd.	835	725	2,200	30-80	16,700
12.	Under W. Hts from Maxton Rd in SW direction	400	350	1,100	30-100	8,000
13.	Under W. Hts at rear of and parallel to Ropewalk	465	390	1,200	30-80	9,300
				26,075		237,345

4. Basement shelters (partially adapted)

Locality	Capacity	Approx. Cost.
1 Leney's Mineral Water Factory, Russell St.	140	40
2 Fremlin's Brewery, St. James's Lane	400	150
3 Stevens Valet Service, Queen St.	160	50

5. Basement shelters (light bomb proof)

Locality	Capacity	Approx. Cost.
Elms Vale District		
1 Mr Haines's land above Queen's Avenue	100	800
2 County School playing field opposite King's Rd.	100	800
3 County School playing field Boar's Head	100	800
4 Church Rd. near Stebbing Down footpath	250	1,800
Folkestone Road District		
5 Mrs Halke's land, Glen Grove, Vale View Rd.	100	800
6 Dover College playing field near pavilion	100	800
Central District		
7 Granville Gardens	250	1,000
8 Clarence Lawn	100	800
9 York Street almshouses	100	800
10 Dover College grounds, Effingham Street.	250	1,800
11 Victoria Park, Laureston Place	100	800
London Road and Castle Estate		
12 Castlemount, near Taswell Street	100	800
13 Castle Avenue	100	800
14 County School for Girls	100	800
15 Alexandra Place	250	1,800
Tower Hamlets District		
16 Astor Avenue	100	800
17 County School for Boys near Hamilton Road	100	800
Barton District		
18 Royal Victoria Hospital	250	1,800
19 Pilgrims Way	100	800
River District		
20 South Road	100	800
21 River Recreation Ground	100	800
22 Common Lane above school	100	800
23 Dublin Man O'War	100	800
24 Kearsney Avenue west	100	800
	3,150	24,200

Having considered this report from the Borough Engineer as well as Bennett's scheme, the final air-raid shelter requirements, costing £250,000, were submitted to the Home Office for approval.

Besides the adaptation of the existing caves at a cost of £740 to accommodate 3,450, the report also recommended extensive deep shelter construction in the form of tunnels to accommodate 22,825 people at a cost of £208,245 as well as adapting sufficient basements at a cost of £24,460 for 3,850 people and surface shelters to protect areas which had no caves. Although it generally favoured the use of existing caves, the Home Office refused to approve or fund the proposed new tunnels project on the grounds that it was too expensive (£10 a head), reminding the council that government policy was to supply Anderson shelters for as many of the general public as possible. Tunnel projects could only be sanctioned if the cost per head was reduced to £4 or less, ie cheaper than Anderson shelters. Apart from the cost there was also a fear that once in the deep shelters people would not return to work! In addition the military did not favour deep shelters for civilians since they would be safe havens for the enemy if there were an invasion.

Public shelters would ideally be confined either to areas where there was insufficient garden space to install Anderson shelters or to accommodate people caught in the street when the sirens were sounded. This national policy based primarily upon Anderson shelters was despite the recommendation from Professor Haldane, an eminent scientist, that deep shelters 30 or 40 feet (9 or12m) underground would be much safer and could be built for £19 a yard. Anderson shelters were cheaper! The 1939 ARP White Paper stated, 'provision of an air raid shelter in or near every residential property should be compulsory'. Only the very poorest, those earning less than £5 a week, could have a free shelter, others had to pay £7 and erect the shelters themselves, usually covered by only a foot or two of earth. They were considered safe except for a direct hit.

Following the government's rejection of the tunnel project, the council conducted a survey that revealed that 6,403 Anderson shelters would be required. On the same day that the first 600 Anderson shelters arrived in August, the Town Clerk, Sidney Loxton, asked the *Dover Express* to publish a full list of the 59 cave shelters, trenches, basements and school shelters available in the town, which it did on 25 August 1939. The list, accompanied by a map, included caves already mentioned plus the cave behind the Masonic Hall in Snargate Street. The basement shelters available during the day were Leney's Mineral Water factory in Russell Street, Fremlin's Brewery in St. James's Street, Stevens Valet Service in Queen Street, Hart's in Cannon Street and the Co-op in Biggin Street.

There was also a reminder that the 18 school shelters mentioned could not be used by the public when children were at school, but could be used during school holidays and on Saturdays and Sundays. This seems strange as children at school when the siren went were told to go straight home! The school shelters were: Roman Catholic in Maison Dieu Road (sheltering 100), Barton Road Infants (92), Girls' and Infants (117), Girls (60) and Boys (78), Belgrave Road Infants (103), Christ Church Boys (56), Old Laundry, Tower Hamlets (220), Charlton Girls (100), River (65), St Bartholomew's Widred Road (104) St. Martin's Girls (79), Boys (96), Albany Place (140), St. Mary's Girls and Infants (34), Old Burial Ground adjoining St. Mary's (68) and Durham Place (138).

Wartime

Following the outbreak of war, tenders were invited, despite the government's refusal to fund it, for the construction of a tunnel to connect Beaufoy's Cave to the Lagoon Cave with an extension from Lagoon Cave to the Tower Hamlets chalk pit to provide an additional entrance/exit at Tower Hamlets Road. This work would make them safe and provide shelter for 660. The use of some voluntary labour probably explains the relatively low cost of £2 8s 4d per head. A proposal to strengthen and provide emergency exits for a number of basements between Ladywell and Beaconsfield Road, making them splinter and blast proof shelters for 658, was rejected. Steps were taken to use caves at the top of Eaton Road and at Elms Vale Recreation Ground with any necessary excavation being provided by voluntary labour. Despite the government refusing to pay £4,385 for the conversion of the water main tunnel from Noah's Ark Road to Union Road and to link it with Edred Road and Widred Road, the council approved the work, welcoming the use of volunteers who excavated an entrance to the water main tunnel shelter at the top of Edred Road.

At this time local authorities were given powers to designate certain shelters for various groups of users. Dover agreed that Barwick's Caves should be primarily for pregnant mothers, mothers and young children.

By 30 October 1939 a number of shelters were ready for use: Athol Terrace, Chapel, Trevanion Street, Winchelsea, Barwick's and the Limekiln Street Bonded Store caves, the basements of Leney's in Russell Street, Fremlin's Bottling Store in Dolphin Lane (314) and St. Martin's in Church Road (70). Winchelsea was the largest cave shelter and also one of the most popular. A number of shop basements were to be strengthened and more trench shelters were approved between Limes Road and Charlton Avenue, off Barton Road (155), as well as a tunnel shelter behind the Regent Cinema in London Road (now the Territorial Army Centre site). Another 260 places were provided at the Shatterlocks trench shelter off Heathfield Avenue.

By the end of 1939 a number of shelters were completed: Laureston Place Cave, the basements of 14 High Street (26), Mackesons at 42 Biggin Street (150), London Road Methodist Church, Harts at 11 Cannon Street (115) and 11 Bench Street (185), Co-operative drapery department in Biggin Street and the rear of River Co-op (80). The Castlemount Tunnel had been extended 35 yards (31m) to accommodate 40 students and staff from Hillersden House in Godwyne Road. The Crabble Road railway arch had also been adapted and trench shelters dug in Barton Road. Arrangements had been made for school children to use the shelters of Leney's in Russell Street and Castle Concrete in Tower Hamlets Road

This story of expanding shelter provision continued into 1940. Where there was no room for Anderson shelters, authorisation was given to strengthen basements in houses whose occupants were entitled to free shelters. Where there was neither room for Andersons nor suitable basements, communal shelters were constructed. Increasing bombardment of the town led to the increased use of shelters for sleeping purposes, raising concerns about public health and the production of a report on the matter, including action that should be taken to ensure suitable standards. In May, it was deemed necessary to gas proof shelters.

By February 1940 the Regent Cinema tunnel, accommodating 200, was completed as well as the basements of the Co-op at 16 Biggin Street (200) and Woolworth at 62 Biggin Street (300). The council agreed to extend the Christ Church tunnel by 60 yards. Since the government refused grants to pay the wages of public shelter caretakers and watchmen, the council agreed to dispense with them.

To complete the air raid shelter picture, there were also a number of sandbag shelters at Chapel Hill beside Buckland Methodist Church (60), beside the Town Hall (65), Tower Hamlets chalk pit (88) and at the rear of 51 London Road (40). Other shelters were located at the Old Forts in Archcliffe Road (18) and Castlemount (165).

In May 1940 the council was told that the Castlemount Cave was now in use as well as basements at 18 Cannon Street (144), John Gale's premises at 15 London Road (114), The Scotch Wool Shop at 54 Biggin Street (68), Greenstreet (Bootmaker) at 18 Bench Street (60) and Bradleys at 3 New Bridge (95). The basement of Buckland Methodist Church was also brought into use sheltering 125 as well as the London Outfitters at 64 Biggin Street (100).

A number of school shelters were also available for public use out of school hours: St. Mary's Girls, St. Bart's Boys, the Roman Catholic School, Christ Church Infants, Belgrave Road, Barton Road, Charlton Girls' School and River.

It was not until October 1940 that the government decided to reimburse local councils for money being spent on shelters, but any expenditure prior to October 1940 would only attract 65% reimbursement. This penalised Dover that had had the foresight to make provision earlier.

Sidney Loxton, the Town Clerk, on 31 October 1940 invited applications for the allocation of sleeping quarters in the Lagoon Cave shelters, although there was no guarantee that all the applications could be met. Priority was given for those with no adequate home shelter who were: mothers and children, elderly or invalid or men engaged on work of national importance. There was the promise of more public shelters being equipped for sleeping soon.

The Duke of Kent, King George VI's younger brother, visited Dover on 28 November 1940 and was taken to see the Civil Defence Secondary Control Centre in the Oil Mill Caves. This duplicated the Control Centre in the Ladywell Police Station and was to be brought into use if Ladywell was put out of action. The Cave Control Centre had a telephone system, large maps of the town and an incident board plus bunk beds and cooking facilities. The Ladywell Centre staff held occasional exercises in the Cave Centre to keep themselves familiarised with it.

The *Dover Express* disliked the way the military had improved shelters it had taken over, whilst public shelters had been allowed to deteriorate. There were calls for better supervision in the shelters to curb antisocial behaviour such as spitting, litter and the practice of booking spaces. Shelters were used for selling looted goods from damaged houses but there were hefty sentences if caught. In December 1940 it was decided that the public shelters needed heating and two stoves per 50 people were provided.

By 1941 the population had dropped to 17,382. There were 18,800 domestic shelter places in Anderson shelters and cellars, 15,000 in public shelters (mainly building basements) and 7,600 deep shelter places in caves and tunnels. Most planned public shelters were in use, but one particular project was denied permission. The council felt that it was necessary to construct additional deep shelters for the River and Kearsney areas in the shape of tunnels between St. Radigund's Road and Gorse Hill with an outlet to Bunkers Hill and another tunnel between Woodside on Whitfield Hill and Pilgrims Way, but the government refused, stating that there were ample shelters in town!

By April 1941 there were new shelters in Priory Gate Road and Dover Engineering Works as well as three of the caves at the Oil Mills owned by the Admiralty. A new tunnel was dug from Westmount to join the Winchelsea Caves. In addition a number of existing caves in Snargate Street – at the rear of the Masonic Hall, the Soldiers' Home, the Shaftesbury and Bushell's Yard – were being opened out and connected to each other. Yet another tunnel was being excavated from the Snargate Street caves under Cowgate Cemetery to Durham Hill. A combination of Tilmanstone coal miners and Civil Defence (CD) personnel were employed with the CD personnel receiving a bonus of 7s 6d per shift per linear yard of tunnel! To complete the picture, eleven communal shelters were erected around the town.

In June 1941 a new tunnel, costing £2,803, was begun, using NFS personnel, to connect the Athol Terrace, Chapel and Trevanion Street cave systems, later known as the Guilford Tunnel. At the Oil Mill Caves an emergency exit was under construction.

Children not evacuated went back to school in October 1941 but only for an hour and a half a day as most of the teachers were in South Wales with their pupils. At Pier Infants' School on the corner of Archcliffe Road cave drill was held each day before lessons began. Their cave shelter was only 10 yards (9m) from the school entrance. Today there is still a cave on the modern Channel View Road behind the P&O building. It is brick-lined, 50 feet (15m) long, 10 feet (3m) wide and 10 feet (3m) high and may well be the cave in question.

The difficult conditions in the shelters sometimes resulted in tragedies: on 23 October 1941 five children were found gassed in a cave on Finnis's Hill. The Benn family had been bombed out four weeks earlier but rehoused on Finnis's Hill. For safety William aged 4, Bertram 3?, Francis 2? and Sylvia 15 months were put to bed in the chalk cave behind the house with a neighbour's child, Ken Duggen, aged 3. An oil stove was lit and a tarpaulin placed over the entrance. When Mum checked at 11pm she found William dead and the remainder suffering from fumes but they survived. In a separate incident another died from a gas fire that blew out.

Christmas 1941 was a dangerous time for Dover and Christmas parties were held for children in the caves. The Lagoon Cave was decorated with paper chains and on Christmas Day 50 children were given a special tea and a present. A similar party was held for 30 children in the Athol Terrace caves.

Of the 16 basement shelters in the premises of local businesses into which people could dash in the event of a raid, one of the most popular was in the basement of Fremlin's Brewery in heavily bombed St James' Lane. Even Woolworth's in Biggin Street offered shelter for 300 in its basement. Often used during shelling raids was the railway arch between Buckland Church Path and St Andrew's Terrace which was protected at each end by sandbagged hoardings.

With most of the construction completed, a major theme in 1941 was the improvement of shelters, including internal blast walls, canteens, heating, lighting, concreting the floors, whitewashing the walls and providing WC toilets wherever practicable instead of chemical toilets. Where shelters were used for sleeping, bunks were provided and allocated. Medical posts were established at the Oil Mill, Winchelsea and Athol Terrace caves. During air raids lasting more than five hours, hot drinks could be provided in the larger shelters at a cost of one penny – although free if no money and clearly in need! In 1941, the shelter at Stevens Valet Services Ltd. was deemed unfit for use and was closed. The shelter at Tower Hamlets chalk pit was also closed for lack of use.

For the rest of the war, most work related to air raid shelters continued to be upgrading the amenities and protection offered. First Aid boxes were provided during 1942. Sixteen full time shelter wardens cleaned and maintained the deep shelters and also prevented any friction; the council, however, felt it necessary in 1942 to make public shelter rules in order to deal with troublemakers. One person was fined £1 by the magistrate for smoking in a shelter. During 1942 the shelter at Fremlin's Brewery was closed as it did not meet new regulations and the London Road Methodist Church sandbag shelter was closed due to the state of disrepair, but Beach Brothers nearby in Beaconsfield Road allowed use of their basement shelter. The Shatterlocks trench shelters were closed in 1942 due to lack of use. Enemy action early in 1943 damaged the trenches at Union Road, while the shelter at the Co-Operative Store in River was downgraded to be used only by people caught in the street as private shelters had been provided for the area. The wooden surrounds of the basement shelter at 15-16 London Road were vandalised, although the culprit was later caught and fined, while an obstruction prompted the council to ensure more police supervision was available at certain shelters to prevent crowds gathering too close to shelter entrances. Military authorities asked to use part of the civilian shelter at Connaught Park for their purposes. Particular concern was drawn to the provision of shelters at school, due to the threat of 'tip-and-run raids' in which enemy fighters had bombs attached to their undercarriages and they then nipped across the Channel solo or in small groups and dropped

(Pic. 145) Sheltering in Dover's Caves

them. Blast walls were advised for the Christ Church school shelter, although the idea was later dropped as it adversely affected accommodation, while Anderson shelters were strongly recommended for St. Bartholomew's, St. Radigund's and River School. The council was especially worried about concentrating children in one or two shelters and advised that small, well-dispersed shelters would be best where there was room.

Snargate Street tunnel shelter system and connecting tunnel to Durham Hill

An interesting letter survives in the Public Record Office (P.R.O.ref HO207/1099) sent on 29 September 1943 to the Chief Engineer, Ministry of Home Security Whitehall regarding a request from the Dover Emergency Committee for permission to line two lengths of the shelter tunnel system off Snargate Street, comprising the Barwick, Bushell's Yard, Soldiers Home and *Shaftesbury Hotel* Caves.

At the back of these caves a connecting tunnel was constructed with an exit tunnel to Durham Hill. The tunnels were 6 feet (2m) wide with roofs roughly timbered. There had been several falls from the roof in the Durham Hill tunnel near the upper end and a portion had been lined with concrete from the entrance to a point where the overhead cover was about 50 feet (15m). The Dover Committee wanted to complete the lining of the tunnel and to line the connecting tunnel at the back of the caves.

The Durham Hill tunnel was usually rather wet apparently, but was comparatively dry when inspected. There had been no recent chalk falls but several places gave trouble when the tunnel was first made. The new lining was satisfactory, but the timber sections were beginning to show signs of fungus and rot. This portion of the tunnel was not bunked and only used as an entrance to the caves; therefore, the regional boss could not recommend concrete lining, but did recommend such lining in the connecting tunnel which was used as a dormitory. The alternative, which would be unpopular, would be to remove the bunks. The connecting tunnel was not originally meant for dormitory use, but as an alternative exit from the caves. Lining cost was said to be £780 for 90 yards (81m).

There was a tragic sequel later in the war. Details were in a report to the Ministry of Home Security Research and Experiments Department entitled, 'A Long Range Shell Incident at an Underground Shelter at Dover' (P.R.O. HO196/29). On 26 September 1944 a long range shell, presumed to be 16 inches (45cm) in diameter and weighing about a ton, damaged an archetype underground 9 inch (23cm) thick, reinforced concrete-lined shelter (900 feet (270m) long 5 feet (1.5m) wide and 5 feet (1.5m) high running under a cemetery at Dover. Original timber board lining to the sides and roof had been replaced in 1942 with concrete. The shell penetrated one of the graves making a circular shaft 38 x 27 inches (95 x 67cm) and 24 feet (7m) deep. The shell penetrated 38 feet (11m) of solid chalk and exploded 7 feet (2m) above the shelter. A compression chamber 10 x 8 feet (3 x 2.4m) was formed and the roof of the shelter was demolished for 12 ft 6 inches (3.6m) with damage to the walls. The velocity of shell was probably 1500 feet (450m) per second.' The report concluded that 9 inch (23cm) concrete lining was about twice as effective as timber lining in chalk. Incredibly, the report omitted the human tragedy: Mrs Patience Ransley was killed in the tunnel, sheltering behind a blast wall. Audrey Hardacre of Beaufoy Terrace, living in Bowling Green Terrace during the war, had a narrow escape on that same day. As a child she used the tunnel regularly to get to the Hippodrome Theatre and Snargate Street. She said, 'When the shell dropped my friends and I were near the entrance at Bowling Green Terrace and had spoken to Mrs Ransley as she passed us going inside.' It was said at the time that lead coffins were seen hanging from the damaged tunnel roof.

It was a bone of contention that the town was prohibited from building more deep shelters whilst more and more underground military accommodation was provided deep in the Castle cliff, particularly as the military importance of Dover attracted the Germans as a priority target. German belief that D-Day would be launched from Dover probably contributed to the considerable shelling of Dover during the summer of 1944 before the German long range guns on the French coast were captured in September.

Despite heavy enemy shelling of the town after D-Day, little work except the routine proved necessary during 1944-45. Shelters at Brookfield Avenue and the sandbag shelter by the Town Hall were closed, while that at the Bonded Vaults, Limekiln Street was handed over to the navy. The entrance to the Snargate Street tunnels behind the Soldiers' Home at 157 Snargate Street was closed to allow the owner to store furniture.

Wartime cave injuries and deaths

Cave shelters did not provide complete protection. Emily Foster, aged 54, died on 4 December 1940. As she entered Scott's Cave a bomb fell causing chalk to fall which killed her. Her body was not found for several days. On 3 April 1942 30 people were sleeping in the underground shelter in Union Road when a bomb scored a direct hit; four of the nine people killed outright were from the same family. On another occasion a 70 years old man, Mr Cleak, was killed at the Trevanion Street cave entrance by falling chalk. Many others were injured, but the proximity of the Casualty Hospital (later Buckland Hospital) helped to save a number of lives. On 1 September 1944 a shell exploded near the entrance of the Lagoon Cave shelter entrance when many people were sheltering there. Buried deep in the debris four bodies were found: Charles Benbow, Mabel Hubbard, Ethel Mills and her four year old daughter, Yvonne. Only five days later three sailors were seriously injured when shells burst close to the entrance of Barwick's Cave where they were sheltering. Later in the same month, as mentioned previously, Patience Ransley, aged 63, was killed walking through the tunnel underneath Cowgate Cemetery when an armour-piercing shell penetrated 40 feet (12m) of chalk and 9 inches (23cm) of concrete.

In many ways Dover was fortunate, surrounded by chalk hills, to have scores of caves and tunnels where men, women and children sheltered during the worst of the bombing and shelling from the French coast – probably the most attacked town in Britain. Shelters kept the casualties low. Throughout the war Dover got on with its life, safe in the knowledge that if conditions got worse there were always the caves. Not everyone used them regularly and some never used them, but they were available.

(Pic. 146) Leaving caves for last time

Chapter 4
Wartime memories

Roy Humphreys in his book *Dover at War 1939-45* relates how Inspector Fenn, head of Dover's Civil Defence Services, took a Canadian journalist on a tour of Dover during 1944, including a visit to the Winchelsea caves, which the journalist reported: '...the caves in which are found the bunk beds of those who seek air-raid shelter and in which a complete emergency hospital has been established. Nursing Sister Banks is in charge of the hospital and she showed me the various places which in an ordinary hospital would correspond to wards, operating room, kitchen and dispensary. Beyond the hospital are the public shelters. A minimum of 800 residents sleep here each night. The centre of the maze of tunnels is called Piccadilly Circus and from it the tunnels radiate in all directions. If need be, the whole population underground could be maintained in health and reasonable comfort for many days. Food supplies for two weeks are kept and in addition sanitary facilities for all purposes. The kitchens can provide 200 hot meals within half an hour.'

Dick Whittamore told the *Dover Express* in 2003, 'Many Dovorians slept in the caves at night, especially the elderly taking in armchairs, oils stoves for cooking and warm bedding – essential in the damp caves. Later bunks were introduced and heating supplied. Canteens were opened and a game of housey-housey was always popular, as was a sing-song if anyone had a musical instrument. The Trevanion caves had a first aid centre manned by the Royal Army Medical Corps. Many properties backing onto the cliffs had their own private caves. Some were furnished and carpeted making them very cosy for the houseowners and their friends. Many literally lived in the caves, but later the authorities ruled that everyone must leave the caves in daylight hours except when there was an air raid. This was for health reasons, but some defied the order. Many had narrow escapes at the entrances to the tunnels when watching dive bombers in action caused by shells landing close by and shrapnel flying about'. Several very wet German prisoners were kept in the Trevanion caves one night before being taken away next morning jeered at by onlookers.' Dick remembered jumping off his bike to shelter in a doorway when a stick of bombs fell. A woman, dashing to a cave, fell over his bike in the black-out, but she didn't seem at all worried about any injuries – only her laddered stockings!

A gentleman at an old folks' cream tea at The Ark Church in 2010 recalled going into the Noah's Ark Road tunnel with his mother and hearing two little girls singing. His mother said, 'Listen to those angels singing.' As a result he thought for a long time that angels lived in tunnels!

Gerald West had a surprise when a photo of him as a small boy appeared in the *Dover Express*. Jean Philpott was pictured comforting younger children in the air raid shelter below the Charlton School playground early in the war. Gerald said, 'That little boy was me and I was crying my eyes out. The picture was used on the front page of the *Daily Mail*.'

Jean Philpott, born in Castlemount Road, remembered an entrance to an air raid shelter used in both world wars at the rear of her parents' garden. When the Second World War broke out the shelter, which could accommodate 200, was opened up again. This meant destroying the summerhouse built by her father with walls papered with his collection of cigarette cards! The summerhouse blocked the entrance to the old shelter which led 60 feet (18m) down into a series of tunnels. 'The shelter was fitted with bunk beds and emergency food storage cupboards, but I think my parents were the only ones to sleep in it during the war.' Other people who used it were those billeted in surrounding homes, most of which were requisitioned to accommodate service personnel.

An old wartime photograph appeared in the *Dover Mercury* in 2001 with an accompanying story. One day in 1945 an American military jeep arrived at Athol Terrace and the GIs on board met three boys (Colin Gibbs aged about five, Michael Culley and Leslie Day each about 12) who showed them round the caves used as air raid shelters. One of the GIs said, 'They told us the story of the blitz and the shelling better than any grown up could have done.' Later, Leslie recalled how they spent each night in the caves for more than two years, 'There was a main passageway through the caves, with smaller off-shoots like cul-de-sacs, containing 20 bunks each.' 'Police officers used to come along and tell us which buildings had been damaged,' added Colin.

Charlie Powell worked for Castle Concrete Co. at the old chalk pit in Tower Hamlets Road from 1934 to 1984 and for 25 years he lived in a small bungalow on the site. He claimed that

(Pic. 147) Tower Hamlets tunnel

the caves in the chalk face were used during the Second World War not only as an air raid shelter, but also as a secret store for rations to be used in the event of invasion. The caves had previously been used as a store for bottled mineral water when the chalk pit accommodated Leney's Brewery mineral water factory, which made use of a pure water stream running underneath. One day a cat disappeared down the remains of a laundry chimney and was lost for three days in the tunnels below until coaxed out with a bowl of milk.

Dick Wilson, who ran the *King William* public house on the corner of Priory Hill and Tower Hill, remembered going to a shelter when the siren went. It was fortunate that he did - his pub received a direct hit.

Mrs Player recalled that her father, John Page, kept a fruiterer's shop during the Second World War at 154 Snargate Street with a cave behind it which was normally used for storage, but during the war was used as a shelter where she slept.

Mrs Beck of River worked at Scott's, the dyers and cleaners in Snargate Street, during the war and remembered that the cave at the back, where the carpets were cleaned, became an air raid shelter for employees and anybody else passing when there was an air raid. During raids people sat on the rolled up carpets. Motor Torpedo Boats were moored in the dock opposite and were a target for German bombers. Sailors were told to use Scott's caves during raids when they were off duty. At the back of the cave was a vertical shaft to the cliff top (probably an old well converted to a ventilation shaft) and this was the emergency exit if the cave

(Pic. 148) Athol Terrace

entrance became blocked, using a basket to enable two people at a time to go up!

Mr Brown worked at Blackmans during the war and sheltered in the tunnel behind the present Chinese restaurant. He had played there as a teenager and also used the tunnel from Tower Hill chalk pit to Westmount. He also remembers an air raid shelter with Disney characters on the walls in Beaconsfield Road under the present fireplace showroom.

A strange find was that reported by Joe Harman who found a tablet with Greek lettering on the wall of the High Street caves. The British Museum translated the inscription which appeared to date from the Second World War. Joe never discovered who the inscriber was and whether he was Greek, the identity of Hebe or the location of Bofors Cafe. The translation reads:

Prayer of the Troglodytes to the goddess Hebe

Oh thou who with biscuits and with tea
Make Bofors caff a paradise for me
Oh Goddess from Olympus sent to Earth
To keep mankind with nourishment and mirth
I would now this war might never cease
That never dawns the hated day of peace
For this will be the signal that recalls
You once again unto Olympian Halls
Oh Hebe are you heartless can you go
And leave me sorrowing here?

John Hornsey spent a lot of time in the tunnels in the latter part of the Second World War, sheltering in caves near the present leisure centre. He recalled, 'As soon as the siren went we took our ready-packed case to the caves. Towards the end of the war we spent every night in the tunnels. There was plenty of fresh air inside. Tea and cakes were served from the underground canteen and I remember sleeping top to tail with my brother on one bunk while mother slept nearby. One night a shell fell on the other end of the cave at Tower Hamlets and the dust came right through the caves. In the Athol Terrace caves bunk numbers are still visible on the walls with signs asking people to give up their bunks to those more needy. Carvings of faces, Union Jacks and names still adorn the walls.'

Mrs Una Weir, born in Dover in 1933 was evacuated to Wales, but, unfortunately, was ill-treated and after three months went to live in Wiltshire for two years with her mother. They moved back to Dover in 1942, but a landmine had destroyed their home in St. James's Street and so they moved in with grandfather at 102 Limekiln Street. They were allocated bunks in the Oil Mill Caves, but dogs were not allowed and so they slept in the adjacent Champagne Caves (Limekiln Bonded Store Caves), using the Oil Mills during the day. Una remembers one large cave with a makeshift stage where Dover's 'Vera Lynn', a girl with a lovely voice called Bridget Cloke, sang; others recited poems to while away the time. At night grandfather used to line up the children to say their prayers before playing his penny whistle outside. The three main caves were lined with bunks and via another tunnel you could look onto the railway track in the railway tunnel. If big guns were stationary in the tunnel, a bad night could be expected. Una remembers the cave toilets with some horror; there were cubicles with no doors, the toilets were oil drums and people performed in full view, although there were separate times for men and women. Groups of women would go shopping together, but on one occasion they could not get out for a couple of weeks and Una remembers delicious currant buns being brought in. Civilians only used the front end of the Champagne Caves as the navy occupied the rest. It was always cold and wet. Una was left for hours sitting in the Champagne Cave when mother heard that the Red Shield canteen had been destroyed where one sister worked and Woolworths hit where another worked, but both were safe. At the back of 102 Limekiln Street there was a small cave and mother decided to use it as a shelter. Dad, on leave from the army, returned home to find all the ivy alight at the back of the house, caused by a German plane crashing, but he managed to drag everybody out. Even now, when Una smells wet chalk, 'I'm back in the caves.'

Harry Tennant worked at the Granada Cinema during the war and used tunnel shelters to get to and from work, entering Lagoon Cave in the High Street, which took him to Tower Hamlets Road. He also used a tunnel 200 yards (180m) long by the back entrance to the old Astor School, which was a short cut to the chalkpit at the top of Priory Hill where another tunnel went on to Winchelsea. There was also a tunnel, he claimed, from the Boys' Grammar School to the rear of Buckland Hospital.

Some years ago Wendy Lynch spoke to her eldest brother, Gerald Sedgwick, and asked if he could remember anything about the tunnels and the war years. He was a child then but had vivid recollections about it. Gerald remembered gran making various cakes, pastries and

(Pic. 149) Time for a Winchelsea Cave cuppa

bread pudding that she used to sell in the canteen. He recalled sleeping in the tunnels on two and three tier bunks and also using them as a short cut to St Bartholomew's school at Tower Hamlets. The canteen was the hub where people would meet and share stories with each other during the raids. Both Wendy's brothers and her mum used the tunnels regularly rather than the Anderson shelter in the back garden. During the war years her father was working away doing salvage work. Gran lived at number 6 and Mum at number 10 Winchelsea Terrace and they were able to get to the caves via their back gardens and down the chalk pit when there was an air raid. The sides of the chalk pit in those days were apparently gentle slopes rather than the steep drop that it is today. There was also a series of steps made from sandbags leading from the garden of the house halfway up the hill. Gerald remembered there were flush toilets in the tunnels and a place where they were able to carry out minor operations. There was also hot and cold running water. In the chalk pit itself there was a decontamination centre, a First Aid Station and an incinerator where the rubbish was burned. There were large wooden doors at the entrance to the tunnels, double blast walls and the gas curtains that could be lowered if there was the threat of a gas attack. He recalled being sent out to a fish and chip shop in Tower Hamlets with younger brother Raymond to buy fish and chips for as many as 20 people some nights when there was no bombing.

On 18 October 1944 King George VI and Queen Elizabeth visited the Winchelsea Caves during their visit to Dover. The Queen was very interested in the underground Medical Aid Post and was surprised that people were still living in the caves despite the end of shelling. She asked, 'Do you still come down here often?' and received the reply, 'We have to Ma'am. You see we have no homes to go to!'

Children's play areas

After the war many of the abandoned tunnels became places for children to play. David Hannent, born in 1946, recalls at the age of 9 or 10 playing with his mates in the tunnels under the castle and finding soldiers' helmets and bullets as well as being chased by the security man. Larry Ellender of River has interesting childhood memories of tunnels. 'One day we were playing in a chalk pit down the road from our school at Astor, when we found a hole in the chalk bank. We could not see the end of the hole as it disappeared down into the darkness. We dug it out a little until the entrance became large enough to enter. After a very short distance we found ourselves in a tunnel that had a tarmac floor and plenty of headroom. The tunnel disappeared down a slope into the dark and we decided to return the next day with torches. For the next few days, we were going deeper and deeper into these tunnels which we found had junctions, with other passages going off in other directions. Occasionally, you would come to an outside door, usually with a small grill-like opening that we looked out of to try to determine where we were. We could never open these doors as they were probably locked from the outside or maybe sealed to prevent access. I could identify at least one of our positions, which would be in a back garden of one of the large houses on Folkestone Road. However, our subterranean adventures were soon to come to an end when somehow the school found out about it and the headmaster, Mr Beal, gave us all the cane! I think that was a bit severe as we were only lads having an adventure, not knowingly doing anything wrong. Why not just express his concerns and tell us not to enter these tunnels?'

(Pic. 150) Queen Elizabeth, 1944

The tidy ruin

Old St. James's Church was a casualty of the war, but rather than demolish it, the ruins were tidied and retained as a permanent reminder of Dover's war damage. The adjacent churchyard was, however, removed to provide a car park for the new leisure centre in the 1970s. Sam Webb of Shepherdswell was employed to clear the churchyard and remembered coming across a hole 6 feet (2m) below the ground with a tunnel going under the cliff. There was a chalk pillar in the centre supporting the roof and it was obvious animals had been kept there for on the walls were rings for tethering animals and a feeding trough had been cut into the back of the cave. So, a result of war one of the many peacetime uses of Dover's caves was revealed.

The future

What does the future hold for Dover's caves and tunnels? Some of the civilian caves will continue to be used for storage, but doubtless their main contribution to local history is over as it is for the many military underground works. Their future is pretty bleak – gradual deterioration and damage by vandals, dangerous play areas for children – and cherished only by underground enthusiasts. The exceptions, of course, are Dover Castle's amazing wartime tunnels which will continue to be a major tourist attraction.

Acknowledgements

As always there are a number of people that I must thank for their assistance in researching and producing this book with my apologies to anybody that I may have omitted:

Underground enthusiasts Barry Stewart, Colin Godfrey, Stuart Kinnon and Paul Wells for information and permission to use photographs;

Paul Isles of Locations Photography for permission to use photographs;

Bob Hollingsbee and John Peverley for permission to use photographs;

Jon Iveson of Dover Museum for information and permission to use Museum photographs;

Bryan Williams of Dover Museum for his help researching photographs;

Kirsty Smith of Dover Castle for her assistance;

John Walton, Steve Carswell and Les Holyer for their assistance;

Former members of Q Dover: Stuart Hall, Charles Hutchins, Roy Hooker, Ken De Coster, George Shepherd, Peter Wall and Peter Pennington;

Ian Lilford for showing me round the Girls' Grammar School shelter;

John Skeggs for showing me round the Barton Road School shelters;

Various cave and tunnel owners for their co-operation;

May Jones for proof reading;

Staff of A.R. Adams for their technical assistance and advice;

And, finally, my long suffering wife, Linda, for her tolerance whilst I worked on this book.

Illustration Acknowledgements

Dover Museum, numbers:	14, 20, 26, 28, 46, 51, 52, 53, 54, 55, 59, 68, 73, 75, 117, 118, 123, 125, 126, 127, 133, 134, 137, 149.
Colin Godfrey, numbers:	99, 103, 104,
Bob Hollingsbee, numbers:	87, 145, 146, 150.
Paul Isles, of Locations Photography, numbers:	1, 4, 5, 6, 7, 10, 11, 12, 13, 15, 16, 18, 21, 23, 25, 35, 40, 44, 45, 47, 48, 57, 58, 61, 62, 64, 65, 80, 81, 86, 90, 91, 97, 98, 105, 107, 110, 111, 120, 128, 132, 135, 138, 139, 143, 147.
Stuart Kinnon numbers:	94, 95, 101, 109, 112, 116, 136, 142, 144.
Barry Stewart numbers:	8, 9, 29, 30, 31, 32, 33, 34, 36, 37, 38, 39, 41, 43, 63, 70, 71, 72, 77, 78, 83, 88, 115, 124, 129, 130, 140, 141, 148.
Paul Wells number:	131.

Sources of Information

Books

Brown R.A., Colvin H.M. and Taylor A.J. *History of the King's Works Volume II* HMSO 1963

Coad, Jonathan *Dover Castle and the Defences of Dover* B.T.Batsford Ltd. 1995

Brown, R. A. *Dover Castle* English Heritage

Platt, Colin, *Dover Castle* English Heritage 1988

Coad, Jonathan *Dover Castle* English Heritage 2007

Hall, Stuart Hall *Q Dover – Dover Castle Unique Communications Centre 1941-74*. No publisher.

Burville, Julia and Peter, *White Cliffs of Dover* Triangle Publications.

Humphreys, Roy *Dover at War 1939-45* Alan Sutton Publishing Ltd 1993

Peverley, John *Dover's Hidden Fortress* The Dover Society 1996

Kent and Sussex Research Group *Kent and East Sussex Underground* Meresborough 1991

Whiteside, Thomas and David, Rupert Hart *The Tunnel Under the Channel* London 1962

Haining, Peter *Eurotunnel, Illustrated History of the Channel Tunnel Scheme* New English Library 1973

Leach, Derek and Sutton, Terry *Dover in the Second World War* Phillimore 2010

Leach, Derek and Sutton, Terry *Our town, Dover 1945-2000* Riverdale Publications 2003

Leach, Derek *Life and Times of a Dovorian Lillian Kay* Riverdale Publications 1999

Official records, reports, articles and papers

Investigation to Locate Bastion Level at Dover Castle by Graham Daws Associates for EH 2000

Western Heights Fortifications: Archaeological Survey Reports by the Royal Commission on the Historical Monuments of England, EH 2004

Dover's Bunker Mentality, Dover, its People and its Tunnels in Two World Wars, a doctorate thesis by Rory Joseph Semple, University of Kent 2005

Dumpy Complex article by Philip Wyborn-Brown Bygone Kent Volume 10 Number 8

Harbour railway tunnel guardroom article by David Burridge Bygone Kent Vol. 9 Number 9

Dover Castle article by Roy Humphreys in Bygone Kent Vol. 26, Number 6

18th and 19th Century Defences at Dover Castle by David Burridge, Bygone Kent Vol. 4 Number 11

Threat Beneath the Waves, article by Nigel Britton, Bygone Kent Vol. 8 Number 4

Lost and Found Underground article, Kent Fire Magazine June 1970

Capel Battery, article by Jon Iveson in Dover Society Newsletter 42, December 2001

ARP Precautions – unpublished research for Dover Museum

Letter in the Public Record Office (PRO REF HO207/1099)

Various private notes by Jon Iveson

Friends of Dover Castle Newsletter Winter 1989

Dover Life Summer 2010

Dover Borough Council Minutes 1914-18 and 1935-45

Dover Express various articles

Websites

undergroundkent.co.uk

kurg.org.uk

underex.fotopic.net

sub-ex.blogspot.com

subterranean history.org

castlekas.freeserve.co.uk

Index of Caves, Tunnels and Shelters
Bold italic type denotes illustration

Aerial Ropeway tunnels 83, *83*
Air raid and basement shelters ... 88, 89, 91, 95, 97, 98, 99, 100, 101, 102, 103, 104, 107
Athol Terrace 78, 80, *80*, *81*, 94, 97, 102, 104, 110, 111, 112
Barwick's Caves 68, *69*, 97, 102, 107
Bay Hill, St. Margaret's 85
Blackman's Cave 72, *72*, 74, 112
Buckland Hospital 74
Buckland public air raid shelter 74
Canterbury Cave 84, 85, *85*
Capel Battery 39, *39*
Castlemount Cave 72, 102, 103, 109
Cave dwellers 82, *82*, 83
Champagne Caves/Limekiln Street Bond 61, *61*, *62*, 102, 107, 112, 113
Channel Tunnels 57, *57*, *58*, 58, 59
Channel View Road 61, 104
Chapel Caves 78, 79, 80, *80*, 98
Croucher's Tunnels 68, *69*, 70
DOE Tunnels 64, 65, *65*, 66, *66*
Dover Castle:
    Annexe Level 14, *14*, 15, 16, 17, 18, 19, 20
    Bastion Level 15, 16
    Canon's Gate 7, *7*
    Casemate Level 9, *9*, 10, 11, 12, *12*, *13*, 15, 16, 17, 18, 19, 20
    Constable's Tower 5, *5*, 6
    Dumpy Level 16, *16*, 17, 18, 19, 20
    East Arrow Bastion 6, *6*, 7
    East Demi Bastion 6, 7, *7*
    Esplanade Level 16, 78
    Fitzwilliam's Gate 5, *5*
    Guilford Shaft 8, *8*
    Gun Batteries:
        Hospital Battery 11, *11*
        Saluting Battery 10
        Shot Yard Battery 10

    Shoulder of Mutton Battery 10, *10*
  Horseshoe Bastion 6
  Hudson's Bastion 6, *6*, 7
  Hurst's Tower 10
  Spur/redan 3, *3*, 4, *4*
  Wells 2, *2*, 3

Drellingore 43

Durham Hill Tunnel *96*, 104, 106, 107

Eastern Docks 35, *35*, 36, *36*

Eaton Road Cave 102

Elms Vale Recreation Ground Cave 102

Esplanade Tunnel, St. Margaret's 54, *54*

Fan Bay Battery 48, *48*, *49*, 50

Fan Bay beach shaft/chamber 84, *84*

Finnis's Hill Cave 91. 96, 104

Fort Burgoyne 33, *33*, *34*

Guilford Tunnel 78, 104

Guston 86, *86*

Hanvey's Tunnel 83

Harbour railway tunnel 66, 67, 89

Hougham Battery *41*, 42, *42*

Lagoon Cave 72, *72*, *73*, 74, 102, 104, 107, 113

Langdon Battery 44, *44*, 45

Langdon Hole 45, *45*, 46

Langdon Lights 43, *43*, 44, *44*

Langdon Prison/National Trust 31, 43

Laureston Place Cave 102

Leathercote Point 56

Long Hill/Roman Road 45, *46*, 47

Lydden Bunkers 42

Lydden Spout Battery *40*, *41*, 42

Masonic Hall Cave 101, 104

Motel/Shaftesbury/Soldiers' Home tunnels 68, *69*, 70, 94, 104

Noah's Ark Tunnel 74, *74*, 102, 109

North Military Road	43
Northampton Street Cave	87
Oil Mill Caves	63, *63*, 64, *64*, 89, 90, 94, *95*, 97, 103, 104, 112
Packet Yard well	67
Priory Hill Cave	94, 113
RAF site, The Droveway	55, 56, *56*
Regent Cinema	74, 102
School shelters/caves	75, *75*, 76, *76*, 77, 101, 102, 103, 106
Scott's Caves	67, *67*, 68, *68*, 107, 111
South Foreland Batteries	52, *52*, 53, *53*
South Military Hill	60, *60*
St. Margaret's Battery	55, *55*
Swingate ROC post	47, *47*
Tower Hamlets chalk pit	102, 110
Tower Hamlets Road	72, *72*, *73*, 74, 93, 102, 112
Townsend Farm Dressing Station	53, *53*
Trevanion Caves	78, 79, *79*, 88, 94, *94*, 98, 107, 109
Wanstone Farm Battery	50, *50*, 51
Warren Halt	60
Waterworks	77, *77*, 78, *78*

Western Heights:

Archcliffe Gate	26, 27, *27*, 29
Citadel	21, 24, 25, *25*, 26, *26*
Drop Redoubt	21, *22*, *23*, 24
Engineers' Tunnel	32
Grand Shaft	24, *24*

Gun batteries:

Citadel Battery	28, 29, *29*
Drop Battery	32
South Front Battery	31, *31*, 32
St. Martin's Battery	29, *30*, 31
North Centre and Detached Bastion	28, *28*
North Entrance	27, *27*
South Front Barracks	28
Winchelsea Caves	70, *70*, *71*, 72, *92*, 94, *95*, 102, 104, 109, 113, *113*, 114